ROMANS
LIFE OF THE JUSTIFIED

John L. Benson

ACCENT
Bible Curriculum

ADULT STUDENT
Bible Study Guide

This Bible Study Guide is designed to assist you in making the
entire Bible your Guide for daily living.

John L. Benson/Author
James T. Dyet/Executive Editor
James E. Burkett, Jr./Publisher
Robert L. Mosier/Founder

Accent Bible Curriculum
Accent Publications
12100 W. Sixth Avenue
P.O. Box 15337
Denver, Colorado 80215

ISBN 0-89636-078-4

CONTENTS

- Paul wanted to preach in Rome because he was burdened about the people. Paul used to be Saul.

- Witnessing

YOU ARE GOD'S SPECIAL SERVANT

1

LESSON SCRIPTURE
Romans 1:1-17

RELATED SCRIPTURE
Genesis 3:15; Galatians 3:6-9;
I Peter 1:10-12

LESSON AIM
To examine the content and power of the gospel; to impress upon Christians that their debt to others consists in sharing with them the gospel.

LEARN BY HEART
"For I am not ashamed of the gospel of Christ: for it is the power of God unto salvation to every one that believeth; to the Jew first, and also to the Greek" (Romans 1:16).

STUDENT'S NOTEBOOK

This column is for the student who desires additional study of the lesson theme.

EVERY DAY WITH THE WORD

Monday	Strangers of Rome	Acts 2:5-12
Tuesday	Exiled from Rome	Acts 18:1-11
Wednesday	Planning for Rome	Acts 19:11-22
Thursday	Destined for Rome	Acts 23:11-22
Friday	Arrival in Rome	Acts 28:11-16
Saturday	Ministry to Rome	Romans 1:1-17
Sunday	Searching in Rome	II Timothy 1:13-18

LESSON PREPARATION

Although the question of who first preached the gospel in Rome may never be settled with certainty, we know that on the day of Pentecost (in Jerusalem) many visitors from Rome were present

5

(Acts 2:10). In all likelihood, those who were converted carried the message of the risen Christ back to metropolitan Rome so that in due time a church developed in the Imperial City.

Roman Catholics have affirmed that the church in Rome was first founded by Peter. However, the Roman epistle never mentions Peter. Had Peter been a resident of Rome and were he the founder of the church there, it is inconceivable that Paul would ignore him, especially since so many names occur in Romans 16. Furthermore, Paul penned Ephesians, Philippians, Colossians, Philemon, and II Timothy from his place of imprisonment in Rome, but he does not mention Peter in any of these epistles. In II Timothy 4:11 he says that only Luke is with him. So, Peter could not have been in Rome.

We learn from Romans 16:3 that Priscilla and Aquila are in Rome. It is probable that they communicated to Paul the spiritual needs of the Roman Christians. Not being able to visit Rome immediately, Paul wrote this epistle in order to discuss theological and practical matters with the young church there.

Perhaps some of the people whose names appear in Romans 16 were present on the day of Pentecost. Adronicus and Junia were converted before Paul (Romans 16:7).

For other references to Priscilla and Aquila, see Acts 18:2,18,26.

THE APPOINTMENT OF THE SERVANT (Romans 1:1-17)

Paul's true greatness is seen in his reference to himself as a "servant of Jesus Christ" (verse 1). He was, in other words, willing to assume the position of a bondslave. Two things can be said of a bondslave: 1) he is owned by a master, and 2) his life will invariably be linked with difficult and burdensome service. As a bondslave, Paul con-

The word "servant" here is *doulos*, meaning "a bondslave." There were more slaves in Rome than free men.

I Corinthians
4:9-13;
II Corinthians
4:8; 6:1-5.

There is no place
for pride, self-
will, or indepen-
dence in the life
of a bondslave.

In verse 1, note
that the words
"to be" are
italicized; they
are not in the
Greek text.

The Greek word
for "gospel" is
euangelion and

sidered himself the property of Christ; he had
been purchased with the sacrifice of His own
blood on the cross. So Paul had done what every
Christian is solemnly obligated to do—yield himself without reserve to the will of his new master.

Paul realized the service of the Lord could be
rigorous. It could demand working day and night,
suffering, tears and privations. It could mean the
bearing of heavy responsibilities and burdens in
connection with the churches. It could involve
misunderstandings and many physical hardships.
But Paul was no longer his own, and his greatest
delight was to do the will of his Lord.

Some Christians consider the demands for full
surrender to Christ's mastery too great to meet.
They think of such service as bondage and restric-
tion. The real bondage in life is service to self. Self
is a never-to-be-satisfied master. Its service is
never complete; its demands are never met; there
is always more to be laid on the altar of this god of
self. On the other hand, surrender to Christ is the
essence of true freedom.

Paul was called an apostle. He was one sent by
the court of Heaven to this world with the message
of the Lord Jesus. He had a divine commission, an
ordination from the nail-pierced hands. He was a
missionary ambassador who represented Jesus
Christ and the affairs of Heaven. As an apostle,
he had extraordinary authority to impose regulations and doctrine upon the churches for all time
through divinely inspired Scriptures.

The word "gospel" is an important word in the
study of Romans. Spurgeon once said, "See what
vitality the gospel has! Plunge her under the wave,
and she rises the purer from her washing; thrust
her in the fire, and she comes out the more bright

for her burning; cut her in sunder, and each piece shall make another church; behead her, and, like the hydra of old, she shall have a hundred heads for every one you cut away. She cannot die, she must live; for she has the power of God within her."

To this message Paul was separated even before his birth (Galatians 1:15). To this message he was called at his conversion (Acts 9:15). To preach it in the regions beyond he was specifically called through the church at Antioch (Acts 13:2). It is this message that occupies so great a place not only in the life and labors of Paul but also in the message of the Roman epistle.

The gospel concerns God's Son; it is centered in Jesus Christ. It is concerned with His incarnation (verse 3) and with His resurrection from the dead (verse 4). The resurrection presupposes the work of the cross and the empty tomb. The gospel says that Jesus Christ is God in the flesh, that He is truly human and the possessor of a perfect but sinless human nature, that he was born of the lineage of King David, that His perfect sacrifice on the cross is indispensable to the redemptive purpose, that He was raised from the dead, and that the man who trusts His substitutionary work as his only hope of divine pardon will be eternally saved. This is the heart of Christianity; it is the gospel.

Paul was separated unto the declaration of this gospel message to a world dying without hope. God conferred upon him the grace of apostleship, and now he felt that it was his lifelong obligation to carry the message to all nations that they might obey the gospel of God—a gospel which calls upon all men to repent of their sins and rest upon the work of Calvary for their salvation.

means "a good message," "glad tidings," "good news." It appears 10 times in Romans. The first good news that ever reached the sinner's ears was the promise of Genesis 3:15. It is sometimes called the pro-tevangelium—the first gospel.

Study the relationship between the grace of God and Paul's special ministry to Gentiles (Ephesians 3:6-9).

THE AMBITION OF THE SERVANT
(Romans 1:8-17)

In Romans 1:8-10 the apostle opens his great heart. He saluted the church at Rome with a prayer that they might receive fresh supplies of grace and peace (verse 7). And what believer does not stand in daily need of these? Then Paul thanked God for all the saints in the church at Rome (verse 8). He assured them that he faithfully prayed for them (verse 9). He took time to pray because he knew the vital role prayer plays in the accomplishing of God's purposes and in the perfecting of God's people. You can't help wondering how much more would be accomplished in the work of the Lord if we spent more time praying and less time organizing.

Paul told the Roman Christians how much he wanted to visit them. He prayed that God would give him a prosperous journey to Rome (verse 10). Little did he know precisely how God would finally answer that prayer. In due time God brought Paul to Rome, but he came in bonds. Nevertheless, he arrived there safely—and at the expense of Rome!

It is altogether possible that Paul desired to extend his ministry to Spain, perhaps to Britain, certainly to Gaul (France). Did he have in mind making Rome a center from which he would work, even as Antioch was in the East? This may have been his plan.

What was his ambition in desiring to visit the Roman believers? He wanted to impart to them some spiritual gift (verse 11). Some interpreters think he had in mind one of the gifts which are

"He giveth more grace" (James 4:6).
"Grace . . . be multiplied" (I Peter 1:2).

Prayer really does change *things*.

Acts 27—28 gives the details of the journey to Rome.

The church fathers indicate that Paul reached the farthest bounds of the West (Spain?). See

mentioned in I Corinthians 12. It is more likely, however, that the "gift" may have been only his help and encouragement in strengthening them in the things of the Spirit (verse 12). Both he and they would be enriched as the result of his ministry among them.

Romans 15:24. II Timothy 4:10 speaks of "Galatia." Some manuscripts read "Gaul" (France).

He desired "fruit" from among the Gentiles of Rome (verse 13). He wanted to win souls there, and he thus expressed his sense of obligation to Rome and his eagerness to preach the gospel there (verses 14,15). He had no reason to be ashamed of the gospel which he preached (verse 16). Well may we be ashamed of our sins, our failures, how little we do for God. But ashamed of the gospel? Never! As one has well said, "Let the skeptic, let the wicked profligate, blush at his deeds of darkness, which will not bear the light, lest they should be made manifest; but never let the Christian blush to own the holy gospel."

The gospel is the power of God. Through the gospel faith springs up in the soul. When God exercises His power in the gospel, it results in the new birth taking place in the believing person. He becomes a new creature in Christ Jesus. What Paul really said was, "For I am not afraid the gospel will put me to shame." The man of God may declare it with the assurance that it will never embarrass him by proving too ineffectual to accomplish what it promises.

The gospel which Paul preached reveals the righteousness of God (verse 17). It explains how sinful men can be righteous in the sight of a holy God. Sinners receive a God-imputed righteousness by faith, not by lawkeeping. The gospel appeals only to faith. It begets faith, and as the Christian matures, his faith increases. The Christian life is a life that begins by an act of faith and develops in faith—"from faith to faith."

NOW TEST YOUR KNOWLEDGE

Answer briefly:

1. What evidence can you cite to prove that Peter was not in Rome? _____

_____

2. What is implied by the fact that we are bondslaves of Christ? _____
3. What was unique about the authority of an apostle? _____
4. What truths does the gospel emphasize? _____
5. What was Paul's intent in going to Rome? _____
6. What is the relationship between the gospel and salvation? _____
7. What is the relationship between the gospel and God's righteousness? _____

FOOD FOR THOUGHT

"The gospel is not something we go to church to hear; it is something we go from church to tell."

—Vance Havner

YOU ARE
SINFUL BY NATURE

2

LESSON SCRIPTURE
Romans 1:18—2:29

RELATED SCRIPTURE
Genesis 6:1-7; 11:1-9; Isaiah 1:1-31;
Acts 17:16-34

LESSON AIM
To illustrate the bent of human
nature when God removes divine
restraints; to find out why all men
without exception need the
righteousness of God.

LEARN BY HEART
"For there is no respect of persons
with God" (Romans 2:11).

EVERY DAY WITH THE WORD

STUDENT'S NOTEBOOK

This column is for
the student who
desires additional
study of the lesson
theme.

Monday	Foolish people	Psalm 74:12-23
Tuesday	Foolish shepherd	Zechariah 11:1-17
Wednesday	Foolish man	Matthew 7:21-29
Thursday	Foolish heart	Romans 1:18-23
Friday	Foolish things	I Corinthians 1:18-31
Saturday	Foolish talking	Ephesians 5:1-7
Sunday	Foolish questions	II Timothy 2:19-26

LESSON PREPARATION

Have you ever attended a courtroom trial where
human life was at stake? In Romans 1:18—3:30
we are in a great courtroom, and the entire human
race stands trial. The Judge is Almighty God,
whose character makes Him eligible to weigh all

Before a man will receive a remedy for sin, he has to find out how sinful he is.

the evidence, hear all testimony, and to act with absolute justice. The charge is that man has consistently broken the laws of God. The defendants are Mr. Heathen, Mr. Moralist, and Mr. Religionist. The witnesses are Creation, Conscience, and the Scriptures. Court is now in session. Let's hear the evidence.

THE CONDITION OF THE HEATHEN WORLD
(Romans 1:18-32)

Scripture recognizes only three divisions of mankind: Jews, Gentiles, and the church of God (I Corinthians 10:32).

These are the crude heathen.

Observe how Paul appealed to the creation in preaching to pagan philosophers (Acts 17:24-29).

The term "heathen" appears in both Old and New Testaments; it is just another word for "Gentile." Everyone who is not a Jew is a Gentile. Today, however, the word "heathen" describes people who are uncivilized and do not acknowledge the existence of the one, true God. This is the sort of people Paul has in mind in Romans 1:18-32. He is speaking of superstitious and idolatrous pagans. The truth is that these people are under the constant threat of divine wrath because they suppress God's truth by their godless deeds (verse 18). God is angry every day with the sinner.

The reason God's wrath is so hot is that the pagan world has turned its back on the revelation which God has given of Himself in creation (verses 19,20). When the heathen see the wonders of the world about them, they have sufficient evidence to know that an invisible person is the cause of the visible creation. This revelation of God in nature has been available to man from the dawn of human history. It clearly points to His attributes—omnipotence, omniscience, omnipresence, eternalness, immutability (unchangeableness).

Sad to say, the information which the pagan

world once had of the being and nature of God did not inspire their gratitude to God for the provisions of sunshine and rain, harvest and gain. They were indifferent to His glorious attributes (verse 21). Their foolish speculations about God arose from minds in which not a single ray of spiritual light shone. The likenesses which they made of the Creator gave abundant testimony to the derangement of their reasoning powers (verse 23).

The society that abandons the worship of the true God can expect nothing but judgment. God removed the divine restraints that had prevented men from indulging in unbridled lust (verse 24). Idolatry leads to immorality. Perversion is the outgrowth of apostasy from God. Women practiced unnatural vices, and the men became inflamed with sexual passion for other men (verses 26,27). Homosexuality is the lowest form of degeneration. Its prevalence in any society marks the moral caliber of that society.

What a fountain of corruption flows in the inner springs of the human heart! When it gushes forth, it runs in many directions. "Wickedness" denotes all kinds of vicious deeds. "Covetousness" is the desire to have more and more. "Maliciousness" is the essence of badness; it is the disposition from which wicked acts come. "Envy" is that uncomfortable feeling people get when someone else receives plaudits and praise. It resents the good fortune of others and would deprive them of it if possible. "Murder" is the premeditated act of taking a human life. "Debate" entails quarreling and contention. "Deceit" is anything calculated to give a wrong impression. "Malignity" gets its special pleasure from injuring others. "Whisperers" indulge in

Thanklessness is a dreadful sin against God. Note how often Paul gave thanks in his writings. Giving thanks is a course from which we never graduate.

According to the prevalence of this sin, how would you evaluate your own country?

Paul equates covetousness with idolatry (Ephesians 5:5).

Jesus said that hate is the equivalent of murder. The killings that occur in war are not in the category of murder.

conversation which is detrimental to the welfare of others, especially secret slander.

"Backbiters" are slanderers and destroyers of reputations. "Haters of God" are those who feel animosity toward God. The "despiteful" are insolent and arrogant against God and man. The "proud" are puffed up in their own conceits and full of disdain for all whom they regard as inferior to themselves. The "boasters" are loud and showy in their pretentions to knowledge and privilege. The "inventors of evil things" are ingenius in crime and swindles. The "disobedient to parents" throw off all parental authority and do not hesitate to abuse parents.

Notice in I Corinthians 13:4-7 how love never commits these crimes.

Compare the list in Romans 1:29-32 with the list in II Timothy 3:1-6.

"Without understanding" suggests spiritual stupidity. "Covenant-breakers" violate all confidences and pledges. "Without natural affection" indicates the absence of all natural feelings of love; they are heartless. "Implacable" means that they refuse all overtures of reconciliation. "Unmerciful" describes them as void of compassion. Even the threat of pending judgment does not deter the sinner (verse 32). Not only does he continue to practice unnatural vices, but he takes unholy delight in the moral squalor of others.

THE CONDITION OF THE MORAL WORLD
(Romans 2:1-16)

These are the cultured heathen.

Not all Gentiles are as grossly immoral and utterly degraded as the raw heathen. There are Gentiles who outwardly possess a high moral code. Many have a sincere regard for morality. Such a man, however, quite often feels self-righteous and self-sufficient. He depends upon his morality to give him a right standing before God, and he frequently makes his own moral code the standard by which he judges other men (verse 1). How significant that the man who condemns others the loudest is often guilty of indulging in the same sins.

God sees the very heart of the moral man. He judges according to reality, not according to mere appearance (verse 2). The moral man is only fooling himself when he thinks that God will not be as strict with him as with the pagan. What he does not seem to understand is that he would have been in Hell a long time ago if it were not for God's patience. God only tolerates the moral man and makes him the object of His goodness in order to give him plenty of time to repent (verse 4). So, his indifference to God's kindnesses makes him all the more blameworthy. In the day when God's wrath spills over, the moral man who has been insensitive to divine forbearance will suffer eternal ruin (verse 5).

The criterion of God's judgment is not only truth but deeds (verse 6). The deeds of a man reflect the attitudes of his heart and mind toward God. The deeds of the saved man are well-pleasing to God, and eternal life will be his portion (verse 7). His rewards will be decided on the basis of his perseverance in good deeds. The deeds of the unsaved, however, are wicked and loathsome to God. Their works betray a heart that has never been transformed by grace. They are quarrelsome and disobedient (verse 8). On the basis of their deeds God will dispense appropriate affliction and misery upon them (verse 9). The judgment of God is not influenced by what a man is according to nature or circumstance. He shows no favoritism

Some commentators believe that verses 1-29 have special reference to the Jews. They certainly pertain to all hypocrites, and Jews as well as moral Gentiles can belong to this category.

Think of what a long stay of execution God in His mercy gave to the civilization before the Flood (I Peter 3:20). Nevertheless, judgment finally fell (II Peter 3:6).

Verse 7 does not teach that anyone can be saved by good deeds. If it did teach this, then it would contradict many other passages of Scripture, for instance, Romans 3:20.

on the ground of personality (verse 11). His judgment applies to all indiscriminately—without regard to reputation, influence, or attainments.

God judges all men according to truth, deeds, and law (verse 12). The Gentiles do not have the law of Moses, but God did write on their hearts certain moral principles which are in harmony with the law of Moses. He will judge them by the inward moral law which was available to them but which they violated despite the warning cries of their conscience (verses 14,15). In judgment God will take note not only of the moral man's actions but also of his inward intents, not just what he does in public but what he does in private (verse 16.)

Conscience is God's watchdog in the soul. —Philips. It is not so much a guide as a goal.

THE CONDITION OF THE JEWISH WORLD
(Romans 2:17-29)

Originally the word "Jew" referred to those who belonged to the tribe of Judah. Later it included the Hebrew race throughout the world. The word was especially in vogue during and after the Captivity.

The Jews gloried in the name that distinguished them from the benighted Gentiles. They put their confidence in their unique relationship to the law of Moses. They believed they alone of the human race were acquainted with Jehovah (verse 17). The law gave them specific knowledge of the will of God. By it they could distinguish between moral right and wrong as no Gentile could (verse 18). It was their privilege to instruct others in the content of the law and thus lead them out of pagan darkness into spiritual light (verse 19). They applied the precepts of the law in order to correct the deficient views of the ignorant (verse 20). Because of all this the Jews thought they were exempt from the judgment of God.

They made the mistake of thinking that possession of the law and enlightenment in the law gave them indemnity from judgment. But Paul told them to take a closer look at their situation. They didn't practice what they preached. They committed the same sins which the law of Moses forbade and which they condemned in the Gentiles (verses 21-23). By not exemplifying holy lives, they exposed themselves for exactly what they were—hypocrites. They might not steal an ox from a neighbor, but they were not above robbing God of His due. They might not take another man's wife, but they thought nothing of lusting after her. They did not bow down before pagan idols, but they had no scruples about sacking the treasures of pagan temples and putting the profits into their own pockets.

The Gentiles had taken note of all of these inconsistencies and developed a distorted view of Jehovah (verse 24). The Jews claimed to be the holy people. What a joke! If their God was anything like them, he must be a miserable character. The Jews were a bad testimony with respect to the reputation of God.

Circumcision was an outward sign of the Jews' special relationship to God. It signified that they were the covenant people and that they had voluntarily committed themselves to observe all the demands of the Mosaic law. The fact that they violated all of the commandments of the law emptied circumcision of its significance (verse 25). As far as God was concerned, they were not circumcised at all; they virtually did not have a covenant relationship with Him because they had not fulfilled the terms of the covenant. They erred in thinking that their relationship to God rested upon an external ritual, and they disdained the Gentiles for

Actually, God was all the more angry with the Jews because they sinned in the face of so many privileges.

See Jesus' interpretation of adultery in Matthew 5:27,28.

What sort of impression of your God do you give the neighbors?

Moses' refusal to circumcise his son meant that Moses refused to identify himself with the covenant (Exodus 4:24-26).

not practicing the ritual of circumcision. But in the reckoning of God, those Gentiles who honestly endeavored to live up to the standard of the inward moral law or who became proselytes and put forth a sincere effort to measure up to the demands of the Mosaic law had the equivalent of circumcision, even though they were not physically circumcised (verse 26). The Gentiles who pleased God despite the fact that they had not entered into the ceremony of circumcision showed up the shortcomings of unworthy Jews who did not please God even though they were scrupulous about externalities (verse 27).

Punctilious attention to ceremonial law does not make a man a true Jew. Descent from Abraham through Jacob does not make a man a true Jew. The physical characteristics of the Jewish race do not make a man a true Jew. In the eyes of God, a real Jew is a physical descendant of Jacob whose heart has been transformed by the grace of God and whose spirit wells up in praise to God (verses 28,29). He worships God in spirit and in truth, not just in ceremonial performances. The Israel of God is not the church comprised of both Jews and Gentiles but saved Jews for whom God will fulfill the physical benefits which He promised to the partiarchs. No Jew is a real Jew until he is a saved Jew. And if he is not a saved Jew, he is as liable to the judgment of God as any Gentile.

FOOD FOR THOUGHT

"Gratitude is a fruit of great cultivation; you do not find it among gross people."
—Samuel Johnson

NOW TEST YOUR KNOWLEDGE

Give short answers:

1. What can we know about God from observing His creation? _____
_____

2. With what two classes of Gentiles does Paul deal in Romans 1 and 2? _____
_____

3. Give four standards by which God will judge men.
_____

4. How did Jewish behavior affect the Gentiles? ____
_____

5. What is a true Jew? _____
_____

6. What purpose did circumcision serve? _____
_____

7. What is the relationship of idolatry to immorality?
_____
_____

8. How did God react to the heathen world that departed from Him? _____
_____

9. God is no respecter of persons. What does this mean? _____
_____

WHY THE JUDGE ACQUITTED YOU

3

LESSON SCRIPTURE
Romans 3:1-31

RELATED SCRIPTURE
Galatians 3; Ephesians 1;
Colossians 2:9-17

LESSON AIM
To prove that every member of the
human race is sin-sick by nature; to
prescribe the only remedy for
spiritual ills.

LEARN BY HEART
"But now the righteousness of God
without the law is manifested, being
witnessed by the law and the
prophets; Even the righteousness of
God which is by faith of Jesus
Christ unto all and upon all them
that believe: for there is no
difference" (Romans 3:21,22).

STUDENT'S NOTEBOOK

This column is for
the student who
desires additional
study of the lesson
theme.

EVERY DAY WITH THE WORD

Monday	Living by faith	Habakkuk 2:1-14
Tuesday	Purified by faith	Acts 15:1-11
Wednesday	Sanctified by faith	Acts 26:13-23
Thursday	Standing by faith	Romans 11:13-24
Friday	Walking by faith	II Corinthians 5:1-10
Saturday	Justified by faith	Galatians 3:19-29
Sunday	Access by faith	Ephesians 3:1-12

LESSON PREPARATION

Jews and Gentiles stand before the bar of
justice. The jury has heard the testimony of three

witnesses—creation, conscience, and law. The evidence is conclusive. Spectators have no doubts about the guilt of the defendants. The Prosecuter is about to summarize His case against the whole human race.

RIGHTEOUSNESS UNIVERSALLY ABSENT
(Romans 3:1-20)

Before the Judge pronounces sentence upon mankind, He permits the Jew to raise any issue which might have a last-minute bearing on the case. In an effort to confuse the matter and minimize his guilt, the Jew introduces four questions. 1) If only inward qualities count—being a Jew in heart and having spiritual circumcision—then what advantage does anyone have by being born a Jew and by submitting to physical circumcision? (verse 1). The answer: Your Jewish connections are of tremendous value to you because they brought you into contact with the Word of God—a privilege which Gentiles never had (verse 2). You enjoyed a special revelation of God's person and purposes. He entrusted you with the prophetic utterances.

Review the content of Romans 2:25-29. The four questions relate to this section.

The fact that large numbers of Jews consistently disobeyed God's Word and thereby brought upon themselves greater condemnation does not discount their advantages, nor does it cancel the promises (verse 3). Unbelieving Jews will, of course, never see the promises fulfilled to them, but God will raise up a remnant of believing Jews to whom He will fulfill the promises. God will show Himself to be faithful to promise despite

God will raise up this remnant of Jews after the rapture of the

22

church. During the millennium He will fulfill to them the promises which he made to Abraham. He will also fulfill the promises to David at this time.

Acts 17:31

Jewish unbelief. God will not spare Jews from judgment just because they had special advantages. Indeed, they will receive greater condemnation for not putting their advantages to good use (verse 4).

Question 2: But why should God judge Jews when their unrighteous behavior only puts God's righteousness into greater prominence? (verse 5). Isn't God unrighteous to judge me for magnifying His righteousness? Answer: According to your logic, God would never be able to judge any sinner, for there is no sin which He cannot use as a means of glorifying Himself (verse 6). If God gets glory to Himself from the creature's sin, that is to His own honor, not to the credit of the creature. The creature is fully responsible for his sins and will be judged for them no matter how God may employ the creature's sin to promote His own purposes and praise.

Question 3: If my untruthfulness sets God's truthfulness in bolder relief, why should I be judged for enhancing His truthfulness? (verse 7). Answer: It goes without saying that you never intended to magnify God's truthfulness. You speak lies in order to promote self-interest. It is none of your doing that God uses your lies to emphasize by contrast His truth. The end never justifies the means. The fact that God brings good out of your evil does not mean that He approves of your evil or that He put such wickedness in your heart. Conclusion: Use all of the deceptive arguments and rationalization you please, but the fact remains that the moral Governor of the universe will condemn Jews for their evil ways.

Question 4: If we have real advantages in being Jews, then we must be better than Gentiles (verse

9). Answer: Absolutely not! You do not enjoy special advantages on the ground of your moral worth but on the ground of God's sheer goodness and grace. You don't deserve these advantages. You are as morally corrupt as the Gentiles who never had these advantages. Neither Jew nor Gentile has escaped the tyranny of sin. Neither has a righteous standing before God (verse 10). Both are irrational with respect to spiritual truth (verse 11). Both are unresponsive and useless (verse 12).

In his natural state no one performs even one good work. Rather, everyone uses the various members of his body as instruments for doing evil deeds without any fear of incurring God's displeasure (verses 13-18). What you have given are mere excuses for your sins, but you are guilty through and through (verse 19). The law has found you out because your conduct has never conformed to the holy demands of law (verse 20).

> Bethlehem was the least among the cities of Judah, and yet by God's goodness this town was the divine choice for the Saviour's birthplace (Micah 5:2).

RIGHTEOUSNESS UNIQUELY AVAILABLE
(Romans 3:21-31)

God gave the Gentiles some 2,000 years and Jews 1,500 years to attain perfect righteousness through law observance. Both utterly failed. Gentiles violated moral law; Jews disobeyed Mosaic law. Obviously, righteousness could not come from lawkeeping of any sort. If sinners are to become righteous, they will have to receive it in another manner.

Although the Old Testament frequently alluded to it, the New Testament alone fully clarifies the principle of receiving a perfect righteousness by

> For the first 2,000 years of history God gave the human family a lesson in faith in the promises. During the next 1,500 years He taught them to repent of sin. Neither measure brought in everlasting righteousness.

faith (verses 21,22). Whoever trusts Christ—regardless of whether he is a Jew or a Gentile—receives the robe of Christ's righteousness. Clothed in the perfect righteousness of Christ, the believing sinner has a right standing before God—a standing which relates to the merits of Christ rather than to human effort. Whenever anyone exercises faith in Jesus Christ, the results are invariably the same: he receives a divine righteousness. Jews as well as Gentiles need this righteousness because both belong to the category of sinners and both continually miss the mark of glorifying God (verse 23).

Because those who are clothed in the righteousness of Christ are truly righteous in the sight of God, God clears them of all the charges which have been brought against them. God cannot justify (acquit) anyone apart from righteousness. Let's not imagine that justification is the declaration which says an unrighteous man is righteous. If God says a man is righteous, it is because that man *is* righteous. The believing sinner is righteous in Christ, "who is made unto him righteousness"; therefore, God makes a formal and legal declaration of the fact of our righteousness.

Nothing in us prompts God to give us a perfect righteousness. The whole process proceeds from free grace (verse 24). Faith is not the cause, the reason, the means, or the basis of justification. Rather, it is the medium or channel through which this provision comes to us. We appropriate the provision by faith. The cause of justification is God, the reason is grace, the means is the redemptive work of Christ, and the ground is the propitiatory sacrifice of Christ.

By means of the ransom price which Christ

Justification does not make anyone righteous. It declares that we are righteous. We are acquitted because we really do have the necessary righteousness. It is the righteousness of Christ which is reckoned to our account (I Corinthians 1:30).

paid, God graciously sets the believing sinner free—this is redemption. On the ground of the substitutionary offering of Christ, God's outraged holiness is satisfied so that He can offer mercy and pardon—this is propitiation (verse 25). God's justice demands an exhibition of His wrath against sinners. At Calvary Christ received the full blast of God's anger against sin in our place. In His suffering and death, Christ endured as our substitute the full penalty which the law must inflict upon the unrighteous. He satisfied the demands of divine justice by meeting all of the requirements of the law.

The word "propitiation" also occurs in I John 2:2. The sprinkling of blood changes the judgment seat into a mercy seat.

In view of this sacrificial offering of Christ, God could righteously suspend His judgment upon the sinners of former generations. God patiently bore with and passed by their sins without exacting a full payment only because He intended to receive such a payment at Calvary. At the cross God gave a dramatic exhibition of His righteous character. There He made all of the legal arrangements whereby He might pronounce believing sinners "not guilty" and remain just in doing so (verse 26). Justifying the ungodly is perfectly compatible with divine justice on account of what Christ did at Calvary in satisfying justice and in providing the legal means for pardoning sinners.

If God had continued to deal only superficially with sin, men would have had good reason to question His righteousness. At Calvary God dealt fully with sin and thus publicly vindicated His righteousness.

God's scheme of justifying sinners denies man all opportunity to take the credit for his salvation (verse 27). The principle of works would not keep men from boasting in human effort, but the principle of faith gives no one occasion to brag. By the doing of deeds no one is justified. Through the principle of faith anyone can be justified (verse 28).

God is one; Jews and Gentiles are accountable

to the same God (verse 29). He does not demand one condition of salvation from one and a different condition from the other. The condition is the same. Both must believe that God provided a perfect righteousness by means of the finished work of Christ at Calvary (verse 30). The condition is faith in Christ, not legal obedience.

NOW TEST YOUR KNOWLEDGE

What word best relates to the following definitions?

1. The act by which we appropriate the provision of righteousness. _____

2. Any act which falls short of glorifying God. _____

3. A deliverance from enslavement to sin by the payment of a ransom price. _____

4. That work of Christ which enables the Father to pardon sinners in harmony with His justice. _____

5. Perfect conformity to the holy standard of God's law. _____

6. A formal and official declaration that a man is righteous. _____

7. The reason why God grants men perfect standing in His sight. _____

FOOD FOR THOUGHT

"Nothing can be honorable where justice is absent."

—Marcus Tullius Cicero

WHAT ACQUITTAL GUARANTEES YOU

4

LESSON SCRIPTURE
Romans 4:1—5:21

RELATED SCRIPTURE
Genesis 12:1—15:21; Galatians
3:6-29; Hebrews 11:8-19

LESSON AIM
To take account of the blessings
which accompany justification.

LEARN BY HEART
"Therefore being justified by faith,
we have peace with God through
our Lord Jesus Christ: by whom also
we have access by faith into this
grace wherein we stand, and rejoice
in hope of the glory of God"
(Romans 5:1).

EVERY DAY WITH THE WORD

Monday	Justified by words	Matthew 12:33-37
Tuesday	Justified in His name	I Corinthians 6:9-20
Wednesday	Justified by faith	Romans 5:1-11
Thursday	Justified by Christ	Galatians 2:15-21
Friday	Justified in the Spirit	I Timothy 3:14-16
Saturday	Justified by grace	Titus 3:3-7
Sunday	Justified by works	James 2:14-26

STUDENT'S NOTEBOOK

This column is for the student who desires additional study of the lesson theme.

LESSON PREPARATION

A certain man in Scotland who had been a member and officer of a church for over fifty years one day made a great discovery. All of his life he had thought that his good works and church membership would take care of his eternal destiny. Then, one day as he was reading, his eyes fell upon these words. "the gospel brings to us not a work to do but a word to believe about a work done." In a moment the truth flashed into his mind. He called his wife, saying, "I see it! I believe it! All of my life I've been working at the keyhole, and all of the time the door has been wide open! All of my fifty years of profession go for nothing, and I get salvation simply through faith in Jesus Christ and faith alone!" Wouldn't it be great if every professing but lost church member would make the same discovery?

" 'Tis done, the great transaction's done."

THE RECORD OF JUSTIFICATION BY FAITH
(Romans 4:1-25)

Job asked the question, "How then can man be justified with God?" (Job 25:4). This is an all-important question, and it can be approached by another question, "How have men been justified in the past?" Inasmuch as the Jews considered Abraham to be such a significant personality in their history, let's examine his situation to find out how he became righteous. Did he achieve it by his own unaided powers (verse 1)? If so, then he would have reason to brag about his own accomplishments without giving any credit to God (verse 2).

The truth is that Abraham believed God, and it was counted unto him for righteousness (verse 3). Abraham took God at His Word. God promised Abraham that his seed would be as numerous as the stars of the heavens. But at that moment Abraham did not have a son. Furthermore, he was at an age when he could entertain no definite pros-

Abraham is Exhibit A in the case of justification by faith vs. justification by works.

Faith is a personal confidence in the God of the Word and in the Word

pect of a posterity. Nevertheless, he believed all that God said, and through faith he received the gift of righteousness which God reckoned or imputed to his account.

If justification comes by works, then justification is a debt which God is obligated to pay. A man who works expects to receive his wages. They are his; he worked to earn them. An employer does the worker no favor by paying him for service rendered (verse 4). Before we were justified, however, we were ungodly. How, then, could we produce acceptable works? Righteousness is a gift of God's grace which we receive by faith and not by human effort (verse 5).

David had the same experience. He was a great sinner, and therefore had no claim upon the divine mercy. Nevertheless, by an act of free grace God put the righteousness of Christ to David's account and gave him a full pardon (verses 6,7). The best thing that can happen to any man is to receive a bestowment of righteousness by grace apart from works.

Someone might conclude that Abraham's justification was based upon circumcision. But when was Abraham justified? Was it before or after his circumcision? The answer is clear: he was justified long before he submitted to this Old Testament rite (verse 10). Circumcision, religious ceremonies, or rites contribute absolutely nothing to justification. Circumcision is not the means of conveying justification or any other grace. Rather, it was a pledge to Abraham that he would become the father of many nations and that an innumerable number of both Jews and Gentiles would become his spiritual heirs through believing the promise, just as Abraham himself believed (verse 11). The

of God. It rests upon and trusts in the work of Jesus Christ— His death and resurrection—as the only hope of salvation.

Justification is an act of God's free grace whereby He declares the trusting sinner righteous on the ground of the substitutionary death of Christ.

fact that Abraham was justified before he was circumcised is proof that Gentiles can be saved without submitting to this rite (verse 12). Those who have the same quality of faith which Abraham exercised will enjoy the same imputed righteousness.

Lawkeeping is not a means of justification, either (verse 13). If the fulfillment of the promises to Abraham depends upon Abraham's descendants keeping the law, then not a single one of his heirs will ever receive the promise, for no one can keep the law (verse 14). The law is not a means of fulfilling the promises; it is a means of exposing the enormity of sin and bringing down the wrath of God upon sinners (verse 15). In order to give us any assurance that the promises to Abraham will be fulfilled, the fulfillment must depend upon the grace of God and not upon the deeds of men. Those who have the same kind of faith that Abraham exhibited will receive the promised blessings (verse 16).

That calls for an explanation about the nature of Abraham's faith. What sort of faith did he have? For one thing, it was faith in the God who has resurrection power (verse 17). It was also a wholehearted confidence that God tells the truth (verse 18). What did Abraham believe? He believed everything that God had spoken and promised. After reviewing the fact that it was humanly impossible for him to become a father at his advanced age, he decided that God's promise outweighed all the circumstances (verses 19,20). Despite all appearances and circumstances to the contrary, Abraham believed he would become a father because God said so. He believed God for the impossible, and that is faith. And to God he gave the full credit for the strength of his faith. He entertained no mental reservations about the fulfillment (verse 21).

It is this kind of faith and this alone which receives imputed righteousness (verse 22). It depends not upon faith itself but upon whom we believe and what we believe about Him. We must trust not just any God but the God who raised up Christ from the dead (verse 24). We must believe that what Christ did at the cross provided the only sufficient basis for God to justify us and that what God did in raising Him from the dead is the confirmation of the value of His death (verse 25). True faith takes at least these truths into account.

THE RESULTS OF JUSTIFICATION BY FAITH (Romans 5:1-21)

An imputed righteousness is not the only benefit we receive in justification. Much more comes to us as the result of justification. We now have peace (verse 1). Men do not make their peace with God. Christ has made peace for us by offering an acceptable sacrifice which reconciles man and God. He has removed the enmity or hostility on man's part and brought us into friendship and fellowship with God. Now that we are on friendly terms with God, we have access (verse 2). He is favorably disposed toward us, and we may approach Him. He has raised us to this permanent status by an act of free grace.

Colossians 1:20

In reconciliation God is the reconciler and man is the reconciled.

Knowing that we have been granted the status of justified persons, we exult in the glory that shall be ours in the future, and we also glory in present tribulations because the sanctifying effects which afflictions now work in us will have implications in glory (verse 3). Troubles are God's means of cultivating our perseverance, and perseverance is the proof that we have truly believed and have truly received a righteousness not our own. The evidence that we really have been justified, in turn, increases our hope (verse 4).

The knowledge that God loves us enhances our hope even more (verse 5). The fact that the Holy Spirit is drenching our hearts with God's love is all the assurance we need that God will never disappoint the hopes we have in Him. And certainly the proof that God loves us is not lacking. Love prompted Him to send His Son to die for us (verse 6). The magnitude and nature of the love of God are best appreciated when we realize that He loved us when we had no ability to love Him in return; in fact, we were quite godless. It is one thing to love the lovely; it is another thing to die for the lovely. It is still something else for someone to die for the ugly and the ungodly, but that is what Christ did for us as a manifest proof that God loved us even in our state of alienation (verses 7,8).

The death of Christ was intended to clear us of the criminal charges that were against us and to bring us into divine favor by removing our innate animosity to God (verses 9-11). If He would do all this by dying for us, just think of what He is doing for us and will do for us out of the resources of His resurrection life!

Before Paul discusses what effect resurrection power has in our sanctification, he compares and contrasts the situation of those who are in Adam and those who are in Christ. One man, Adam, is the cause of the ruin which has come to the human race. God views every member of the human family as having sinned in Adam (verse 12). This truth may not appeal to our sense of justice or to our power of reason. We just have to take God's Word for it. In the divine reckoning, when Adam sinned, we sinned. The fact that all die is proof that all sinned. Infants do not have the opportunity to commit voluntary acts of transgression, and yet they die because they have sinned. It must be, then, that they sinned in Adam. Likewise, all of the people between Adam and Moses died even though they did not commit voluntary acts of disobedience against the express commands of God. All during this period God did not give any express commands. It must be, then, that these people died because they sinned in Adam (verses 13,14).

The effect of one man's trespass was terrible: the mass of mankind died. The grace of God at work, however, has a much greater effect, for it has the power to restore all that Adam ruined in his fall (verse 15). The superabounding grace of God brings us into blessings which Adam never did possess, even in his unfallen estate, and which he had no right to expect. By the one sin of one man have come judgment and condemnation, but the free gift of righteousness takes into account the many sins of many people (verse 16).

All whom Adam represented and who were contained in him are condemned with him and in him because they are guilty of his sin. On the other hand, all whom Christ represented and who are in Him are justified because His righteousness has been imputed to their account (verse 18). Christ's obedience is the basis on which those who are in Him are constituted righteous people. By the same token, Adam's disobedience is the basis on which

with both in considerable detail.

Adam was not confirmed in righteousness, as his fall proves. But those whom Christ justifies are confirmed in righteousness. It is impossible that they should forfeit their righteous status.

34

those who are in him are constituted sinners (verse 19). Nothing which the believer does or does not do makes him righteous; he is righteous in Christ. Nothing which the sinner does or does not do makes him a sinner; he is a sinner in Adam.

The law of Moses entered the picture, not as a means of justifying sinners but as a means of showing sinners how sinful they were (verse 20). Although the law exposed the exceeding sinfulness of sin and uncovered many transgressions, the mighty grace of God is fully sufficient to overwhelm the deluge of iniquity. Sin reigned in the sense that it exercised absolute sway over all of the descendants of Adam and predominated over the soul of every man. The result is death and eternal misery. But grace is far more influential in its effects, for it exercises a royal power to secure sinners against condemnation and death and bring them eternal life through the Lord Jesus Christ (verse 21).

FOOD FOR THOUGHT

"I believe the promises of God enough to venture an eternity on them."
—Isaac Watts

NOW TEST YOUR KNOWLEDGE

Fill in the blanks:

1. Adam's sin brought _____, _____, and _____ to the whole human family.

2. Christ's obedience unto death provides _____, _____ and _____ to all who believe.

3. Justification affords us _____, _____, _____, _____, and _____.

4. Abraham's case shows that neither _____ nor _____ is a means of justification.

5. _____ and _____ were the human obstacles that stood in the way of Abraham receiving the fulfillment of the promise.

6. Christians glory in _____, _____, and _____.

7. God promised Abraham that he would become _____ and _____.

8. By what means did God deliver us from our offenses? _____. By what means did He assure us of the merit of Christ's death? _____.

9. We are justified by _____, by _____, and by _____.

10. What two powers reign? _____ and _____. Which has ultimate triumph? _____.

YOU CANNOT
GO ON SINNING

5

LESSON SCRIPTURE
Romans 6:1-23

RELATED SCRIPTURE
Galatians 2:19,20; 3:26-29;
Colossians 2:10-15; I Peter 4:1,2

LESSON AIM
To encourage the Christian to make
good in his experience what God
says of his estate in Christ.

LEARN BY HEART
"For sin shall not have dominion
over you; for ye are not under the
law, but under grace"
(Romans 6:14).

STUDENT'S NOTEBOOK

This column is for
the student who
desires additional
study of the lesson
theme.

EVERY DAY WITH THE WORD

Monday	All manner of sin	Matthew 12:31-37
Tuesday	Wages of sin	Romans 6:14-23
Wednesday	Law of sin	Romans 8:1-4
Thursday	Strength of sin	I Corinthians 15:51-58
Friday	Man of sin	II Thessalonians 2:1-12
Saturday	Deceitfulness of sin	Hebrews 3:7-19
Sunday	Pleasures of sin	Hebrews 11:23-29

LESSON PREPARATION

This story is
cited in the book
Born Crucified.

During the Civil War it was evidently a legal
practice to get a substitute to take another man's
place in military service. Dr. L. E. Maxwell tells of
George Wyatt, whose name was drawn to go to

the front. He had a wife and six children. But a young man by the name of Richard Pratt offered to go in his stead. He was accepted and joined the ranks, bearing the name and number of George Wyatt.

In due time Pratt was killed in action. The authorities later sought again to draft Wyatt into service, but he protested, entering the plea that he had died in his identification with Pratt as his substitute. Wyatt was exempted as beyond all the claims of law and further military service.

Death frees us of all obligations.

This interesting episode graphically illustrates the Biblical truth of the believer's union or identification with Christ. When He died, we died with Him; and in our death with Christ neither sin nor the law has any further claim on us.

CHRISTIANS ARE DEAD TO SIN
(Romans 6:1-10)

Paul has proved his point that justification comes by faith without the works of the law. But has he proved more than he intended? Some of his critics said that his doctrine of justification would embolden believers to sin all the more, out of a mistaken notion that the more they sinned the more opportunity they would give God's grace to show its supremacy (verse 1). The very thought is repugnant to Paul. He denies that justification by faith aids and abets the sinner (verse 2). Then in the next few verses he shows why it is absolutely impossible for any truly justified person to continue in sin. His first point is that all believers without exception died to sin. This expression, "dead to sin," does not mean that any Christian

Antinomians take the unscriptural attitude that because we are under grace, we do not have to conform to any regulations. Break every rule in the book, for grace will always come to our rescue. You can find the answer to such blasphemy in Titus 2:11-14.

stops sinning; nor does it mean that God has made provisions for us which make it possible for us to stop sinning if only we would avail ourselves of the provisions. It simply means that every believer has been cut off from his former relationship to sin.

You don't have to read very far in Romans 6 to find out what our former relationship to sin involved. In verse 6, we learn that we served sin as a slave served his master. This same idea occurs repeatedly throughout the chapter. In verse 14, we learn that sin had dominion over us. It exercised the power and authority of a reigning monarch. Sin was king of our lives. When Paul says that we died, he means that we have been severed from that relationship in which sin absolutely dominated every fiber of our being. Such a condition of tyranny is no longer true in the experience of any genuine Christian, no matter how carnal a Christian may be or how backslidden he may be.

The next item is to explain when we died or in what sense we are dead. Every believer died when Christ died. In His death He represented us. We are identified with Him in His death. This is the kind of inseparable and intimate union we enjoy as the result of being in Christ. There is only one explanation of how we came to relate to Him in this unique manner: the baptizing work of the Holy Spirit placed us into Him. He is the Head of the living organism, and we are the body. The Head experienced death, burial, and resurrection, and the body participated also in these events (verse 3). We were all baptized into His death, and when a Christian goes down into the waters of baptism, he depicts his spiritual union with Christ.

The Father raised Christ from the dead, and

Throughout this lesson you will note such terms as dominion, thralldom, enslavement, mastery, sovereign rule, etc. These words describe the absolute power which sin has over non-Christians. None of these terms is appropriate to describe the present power of sin in the Christian's life.

because we are in Christ, we shared in His resurrection. His life was characterized by resurrection power, and our lives are characterized by resurrection power. This means that the same power which raised Him from the dead now works in all believers to enable them to conform to a new standard and manifest a new conduct (verses 4,5). This fact ought to be enough to convince us that justification by faith does not make allowances for Christians to go on living as they did before they received Christ by faith. Like Christ in His resurrection, we have entered upon a different quality of life. The believer's union with Christ makes his continuance in sin not only unlikely but impossible.

Paul thinks of sinful human nature as "the body of sin" (verse 6). By this he means a highly organized kingdom over which sin reigns as king. This inward mass of corruption is the source and seat of all our sinning. Just as long as this governing power exercises absolute sovereignty in a man's life, that man will do nothing but sin. That power has to be broken. That tyrant has to be deposed. That old man must loosen his grip upon the reins of our reason, emotions, and will. Who is sufficient for these things? God alone in His undiluted majesty and might.

The "old man" is a picturesque designation for our inborn tendency to sin. Paul says that our old man was dealt with when Christ was crucified. To be sure, those sinful inclinations are not dead, slumbering, or inactive. But they are under a judicial sentence of death which guarantees that they will be annihilated eventually, and meanwhile they are greatly limited in their movements because they are pinned to a cross. In that situa-

The whole point of Romans 6 is not the idea that these provisions make it possible for us not to continue in sin. The thought of the passage is that these provisions make it impossible for us to continue in sin.

"Old Man" is a figure of speech—a personification—which calls attention to all that distinguishes a natural man. It is the utter corruption of human nature as it came to be in the fall of Adam. It is not a literal person inside of us who entices us to sin.

Be careful! Indwelling sin has not lost all of its power any more than the devil lost all of his power in his demotion. He still goes about like a roaring lion trying to convince people that he retains the same authority that he originally had, and in the process he inflicts terrible injuries. Indwelling sin puts on the same performance.

tion they are incapable of terrorizing and tyrannizing us to the extent they once did. At the cross Christ took steps to put a limit upon the operations not only of the devil but upon the sin nature of believers.

Our new relationship to sin includes being justified from sin (verse 7). In the death of Christ we have been acquitted from the guilt of sin and consequently removed from the penalty which sin demands. We are no longer answerable to sin; it has no authority to order us around. Sin may put on airs of still sitting upon the throne of our lives, but the truth is that God has dethroned this despot and stripped him of many of his powers. Sin can no more dominate the life of any Christian than a slaver can lord it over a dead slave. Sin is as powerless to dominate in the Christian as death is powerless to bring the resurrected Christ back to the grave (verses 8,9).

Our experience parallels that of Christ in many details. He too died to sin (verse 10). His death placed Him into an entirely different relationship to sin. Before His death He bore our sins on the rugged tree; He paid the penalty which sin demanded. Now sin does not have the same claim on Him as it did before. On the cross He dealt fully with the sin question. Now He has entered a state in which dealing with sin is no longer necessary or possible. Likewise, we who are in Christ died to sin. We no longer sustain the same relationship to it that we once did. It no longer rules us. It vexes us, distresses us, influences us, and tries vainly to get the mastery over us, but it cannot dominate us.

CHRISTIANS ARE ALIVE TO SERVICE
(Romans 6:11-23)

Here is the undeniable fact: you are dead to your former relationship to sin. Now what are you going to do about it? God has said it; it is actually true. Your responsibility is to count on it (verse 11). Paul does not say that we should act *as if* we were dead to sin, nor does he instruct us to *become* dead to sin. He tells us to act as those who are dead "indeed." Our death to sin is a reality to be reckoned with, and our new life unto God is equally a fact to appreciate.

Because we are dead to sin and because sin no longer reigns in us, we must not permit it to reign (verse 12). The fact of our deliverance from the dominion of sin is the incentive we need to refuse to acknowledge the rule of sin. We give no consent to its claims and pay no heed to its demands, for sin is no longer a sovereign to command our obedience. Sin is still present and powerful; otherwise, we would never experience a lustful feeling. But sin is no longer an absolute dictator.

We have no reason or right now to place the physical faculties of our body at the disposal of the fallen monarch (verse 13). It would be folly to enlist in the old tyrant's service and lend our bodily members again for sin to use as weapons in the cause of unrighteousness. Rather, we who are alive unto God present ourselves—all that we are—to God for Him to employ all of our faculties as weapons in the cause of righteousness.

When we speak of the fallen monarch and the old tyrant, we do not refer to Satan; we are talking about the power which inborn and indwelling sin once exercised in us.

Another reason why sin cannot have dominion over any Christian is that every Christian belongs to a new regime. We are all under the regulating power of grace (verse 14). God in grace has broken

42

the mastery which sin had over us. Sin is no longer lord and master because God's grace at work in the saved soul will not tolerate it. Grace is a new and sovereign power which delivers us from servitude to sin but does not so overwhelm the soul that the Christian can no longer sin.

People who think they can go on sinning as they did before their conversion entertain a deficient view of that grace of God which sanctifies His people (verse 15). If they are not really unsaved, at least they are ignorant of the real nature of God's grace. They need to consider that whatever master rules them is the evidence of their true state. If they are still enslaved to sin and willingly obeying all of its dictates, they are manifestly unregenerate, no matter how loudly they profess to be saved (verse 16).

This sad situation was not true of the Roman Christians. Paul had no doubts about which Master they served (verse 17). They yielded wholehearted obedience to the instructions of a new King—their obedience being the proof of a new relationship to sin and a new relationship to God in Christ. Their transference from the miserable slavery of sin to the joyous service of God was obvious. Emancipation from the old potentate left them free to serve Christ (verse 18). They had formerly rendered voluntary obedience to sin's demands for impurity and iniquity. Now they must give the same willing obedience to the Spirit's call to sanctification (verse 19). Holiness is the aim of the liberated Christian.

All of those who are slaves to sin are utterly destitute of any righteousness (verse 20). Such a description cannot apply to any Christian now. This was our former condition. In justification

Is anything more insulting to grace than to imagine that we have been freed from our former sin-master only to become our own master and do as we please?

Notice the relationship of faith to obedience in Romans 1:5 and 16:26.

43

God declared us to be righteous; in sanctification God is making us righteous. All who are justified are being sanctified, and this precludes the possibility that any Christian is still the servant of sin. We have entirely new feelings about unrighteousness. We cannot think of our past performances without feeling ashamed (verse 21). And we shudder to think of how those unrighteous deeds of ours were taking us down the broad road which leads to destruction.

But now—what a difference, and what grace to make it so—having released us from sin's thralldom, God has engaged us in His employment with the result that we are for the first time able to produce the kind of deeds which have holiness in view (verse 22). The issue of such fruit is life everlasting—not as wages for service but as a free gift (verse 23). The righteous deeds of the servants of God are not meritorious in themselves; they make us deserving of neither eternal life nor reward. Eternal life is God's gift to us and the awards at the end of life's service are a boon of His grace. The servants of sin, however, earn their wages down to the last penny.

> What would you say to a Christian who says that God has burned out all the traces of the old nature in him?

FOOD FOR THOUGHT

"Victories that are easy are cheap. Those only are worth having which come as the result of hard fighting."
—Henry Ward Beecher

Answer true or false:

1. The doctrine of justification by faith emboldens Christians to sin all the more.

2. Only those Christians who yield completely to God are dead to sin.

3. All Christians, regardless of their spiritual condition, have been freed from the domination of sin.

4. Sanctification follows justification just as surely as day follows night.

5. God holds out to every Christian the possibility of never sinning in this life.

6. The baptizing work of the Spirit unites every Christian to the crucifixion, death, burial, and resurrection of Christ whether the Christian knows this fact or not.

7. The sinful inclinations which we received from Adam will die in us if we seek to die daily.

8. Christians have the power to dethrone the tyrant of sin in their lives.

9. The only power which can depose the tyrant of sin in the life of anyone is God's almighty power.

10. Christ died to sin in the sense that He struggled with the power of indwelling sin and overcame it.

YOU FACE A
LIFELONG FIGHT

6

LESSON SCRIPTURE
Romans 7:1-25

RELATED SCRIPTURE
Galatians 5:17; II Timothy 4:7;
James 1:13-16; I Peter 4:1-6.

LESSON AIM
To prepare Christians for a lifelong
battle with the power of indwelling
sin; to assure them of the final outcome lest they lose heart in the
fight when they suffer temporary
defeats.

LEARN BY HEART
"For I know that in me (that is, in
my flesh,) dwelleth no good thing:
for to will is present with me; but
how to perform that which is good I
find not" (Romans 7:18).

EVERY DAY WITH THE WORD

Monday	Will of the flesh	John 1:1-13
Tuesday	Motions of the flesh	Romans 7:1-6
Wednesday	Works of the flesh	Galatians 5:16-21
Thursday	Desires of the flesh	Ephesians 2:1-10
Friday	Sins of the flesh	Colossians 2:9-23
Saturday	Filth of the flesh	I Peter 3:18—4:6
Sunday	Lust of the flesh	I John 2:12-17

This column is for
the student who
desires additional
study of the lesson
theme.

LESSON PREPARATION

What is your first reaction to a sign that reads
"Keep off the Grass"? When you see a traffic sign
"Speed Limit 20 mph," do you try to get away

with driving 30 mph? When you see a sign which says "Speed Checked by Radar," do you resent the fact that you don't have even a sporting chance to break the law? Laws have a way of bringing to the surface our natural dislike for anything and everything that restrains us from doing as we please regardless of the consequences to ourselves or to others.

Lawlessness is one of the traits of Adam's nature in us.

AN EXTERNAL LAW
(Romans 7:1-13)

In Romans 6:14, Paul announces that Christians "are not under law." But for the moment he does not develop the subject because he is concentrating on explaining how we are dead to sin. In Chapter 7, verses 1-13, he amplifies the subject of our death to law. Death to law is as important as death to sin because as long as we are related to the law's demands, our sinful nature reacts violently to the restraints which law puts upon it. You can't be dead to sin if you are not dead to law. In the case of every Christian, however, he is dead indeed to law and therefore to sin.

In the book of Romans, the word "law" does not always refer to the same thing. Sometimes it means Mosaic law. It can also refer to any operating principle or even the moral law which God has written on the human heart.

How long does a person come under the jurisdiction of law? Common sense tells us that everyone is obligated to it "as long as he liveth" (verse 1). The marriage contract aptly illustrates this principle. According to divine and civil law, how long is a woman obligated to her husband? "As long as he liveth" (verse 2). What is the only circumstance which can free her from the marriage bond? Death—either her death or her husband's.

In the eyes of the law death cancels the woman's status as a wife. While her husband is living she cannot marry another man without committing adultery (verse 3).

The analogy of the marriage relationship is plain. We were married, as it were, to law—a relationship which bound us to law throughout our lifetime. Law was our first husband, and we were not free to be joined to Christ in holy intimacy (verse 4). Only a death could set us free. That death occurred. It was not the death of our first husband, the law, but *our* death that severed us from the law's demands. We died in the death of Christ. Through the offering up of His body to crucifixion, He broke the hold which law maintained on us. Our relationship to the law resulted in no spiritual produce. Our relationship to Christ results in "fruit unto God."

Before we were joined to Christ, everything that issued from our lives was sinful. We produced only the kind of deeds that deserved the penalty of death (verse 5). Our works were unqualifiedly sinful because they sprang out of those sinful impulses which we inherited from Adam. We were in the flesh; which means we were unregenerate and dominated by what we were by nature.

That sad state was our lot before we became dead to sin and to a law that irritated our sinful nature. Now the Holy Spirit supplies inwardly what the law demanded but could not provide. Our service and works no longer derive entirely from what we are by nature; they spring up as the result of what the Holy Spirit produces in us by His grace and power (verse 6).

The fact that the law cannot enable anybody to do what it requires is no reflection on the law. God

The marriage relationship is descriptive not only of Jehovah's intimacy with Israel but of Christ's union with the church. See the NSRB, note 1, page 920.

Of course, even the law will not have this effect unless the Holy Spirit effectively applies the principles of the law to the conscience. It is the Spirit that wounds the conscience with the weapon of law.

never intended that the law should provide enabling grace. The law served a different purpose. It was God's instrument for bringing the sinner under conviction by showing him the real nature and extent of his sin. Without the Tenth Commandment Paul would not have realized that his inward desire for the things God had forbidden was sin (verse 7). He would have remained blind to the corruption of his heart if the law had not exposed it. But that was not the worst of it. As soon as he saw that the law imposed restraints upon his inward sinful desires, he felt an uncontrollable urge to break out of those restraints and commit all kinds of sins (verse 8).

Before this experience Paul had no idea of how sin seethed in his heart. He supposed he was righteous, but he was living in a fool's paradise. The prohibition of the law got a violent reaction from his sinful nature, and he then saw himself as a dead man—not dead *to* the law but slain *by* the law (verse 9). The law which promised eternal life and happiness to those who perfectly conformed to it proved to be an instrument of death (verse 10).

Indwelling sin had deceived Paul into thinking that he was right with God on the ground of law-keeping. But when he came to realize the spirituality of the law, all of his self-assurance went down the drain (verse 11). It was not the fault of the law, for the law is holy, just, and good (verse 12). But the law did have a result just the opposite of what Paul had expected. It pronounced the death sentence upon him because he had not really conformed to what the law demanded of his attitudes and dispositions. The law showed him how exceedingly sinful he was (verse 13).

By the spirituality of the law we mean that the law requires inward holiness and purity. It demands that our character conform to God's character.

49

OUR POST-CONVERSION RELATIONSHIP TO AN INTERNAL LAW
(Romans 7:14-25)

In view of the spirituality of the law, Paul knew that he was carnal (verse 14). Notice that he did not say, "I *used to be* carnal." Although verses 14-25 represent Paul's experience as a converted and regenerate man, he was still carnal. Something in him still resented the restraints of law. Something in him still responded to outward solicitation to do evil. That "something" was indwelling sin. After a person's conversion indwelling sin still struggles for the mastery it enjoyed before conversion. Regeneration does nothing to change the nature of indwelling sin. The old nature—the sinful inclinations which we received from Adam—is still sold out to sin. It is as corrupt as ever.

It is the presence and power of indwelling sin that accounts for the fact that, determine as we will, we do not invariably practice what is pleasing to God. We feel an inward revulsion for the sinful things we do, and yet we continue to do them (verse 15). In one part of our inmost being we approve of the righteous demands of the law (verse 16) and disapprove of our contrary nature (verse 17). But despite our delight in God's law and our detestation for what we are by nature, we never arrive at a point in our Christian life when we are no longer troubled by the uprisings of indwelling sin.

There is nothing good in what we are by nature apart from grace. The flesh nature is exactly what it was when we were first saved (verse 18). And it is the flesh nature which interferes with our holy ambitions so that our performance never measures

From lesson 5, remember that indwelling sin no longer has mastery over any Christian, but it still longs and labors for mastery. It gives us no rest in its endeavors.

"No good thing" is a categorical and unqualified statement. Let's give it the full force that the

Spirit intended. Whatever we do in the energy of the flesh is not only worthless but wicked. This is not to say, however, that the Christian does nothing good. In the Spirit's strength he does much that is good and he makes progress in doing more and more good. But the only good in us is that which the power of the Spirit puts in us. We don't have it naturally.

up to our resolutions. We continue to will to do good and fail; we continue to will to avoid the bad and fail (verse 19). Every effect must have a sufficient cause. What is the ultimate cause of our failure? Indwelling sin (verse 20)! But we must beware of taking no blame to ourselves. We cannot shift the whole responsibility to the indwelling principle of sin and personally disavow all moral accountability. *I,* not my sin nature, do the evil. *I,* not my flesh, do not do the good. *I,* not my old man, serve the law of sin. We are fully responsible for everything that indwelling sin prompts us to do.

Indwelling sin is so real, so powerful (not all-powerful or even dominant), and so permanent that Paul calls it "a law" (verse 21). It is always present and has at least some influence on everything we think, feel, and will. It is a law, principle, power, force that has declared an all-out war against everything we are by grace (verse 23). By grace we delight in God's law; by nature we resist it. Two opposing principles are at work in every Christian: the power of indwelling sin and the power of the indwelling Spirit. Indwelling sin drags down our mind to base objects; the indwelling Spirit counteracts the downward trend.

Every Christian feels this raging war in his consciousness. The fight sometimes has a brief lull; at other times it gains the momentum of pitched battle. The internal conflict causes us the severest anguish (verse 24). We cry for deliverance from the presence of indwelling sin. And in our moments of deepest misery, we remember the promise that when Christ comes, He will eradicate every trace of Adam in us (verse 25).

Meanwhile the war is on. There is no end to the

conflict as long as we are in this world. Realization of the final victory is not yet; it belongs to the future. Even the holiest saint on earth has not attained it yet. In our most advanced stage of progressive sanctification we shall still be serving the law of God with the renewed mind and at the same time serving the law of sin with our inborn and unaltered carnality. Dig in for a long fight!

NOW TEST YOUR KNOWLEDGE

Fill in the blanks:

1. Every Christian is dead to _____ and _____.

2. Only _____ cancels the marriage relationship.

3. Before conversion all of our impulses were _____.

4. _____ exposes the nature and extent of our sinfulness.

5. _____ is contrary to every godly impulse we feel.

6. Indwelling sin will strive against the restraints of the Holy Spirit for _____.

7. _____ is a term which refers to the sinful inclinations we received from Adam.

FOOD FOR THOUGHT

"The biggest trouble with sin is the I in the middle of it."

—Eld

YOU ARE GOD'S SON AND HEIR

LESSON SCRIPTURE
Romans 8:1-25

RELATED SCRIPTURE
Genesis 3:18,19; I Corinthians 3:1-3;
Galatians 4:1-7; Ephesians 2:1-10

LESSON AIM
To inspire hope in what Christ will
do for us.

LEARN BY HEART
"For as many as are led by the
Spirit of God, they are the sons of
God" (Romans 8:14).

STUDENT'S NOTEBOOK

This column is for the student who desires additional study of the lesson theme.

EVERY DAY WITH THE WORD

Monday	Spirit of counsel	Isaiah 11:1-10
Tuesday	Spirit of truth	John 16:12-24
Wednesday	Spirit of holiness	Romans 1:1-7
Thursday	Spirit of promise	Ephesians 1:1-14
Friday	Spirit of power	II Timothy 1:6-14
Saturday	Spirit of grace	Hebrews 10:26-39
Sunday	Spirit of glory	I Peter 4:12-19

LESSON PREPARATION

How many other definite commands can you find in Romans 1—7?

Romans 6—8 is a unit. Romans 6 commands us to reckon ourselves dead to sin and alive unto God (verse 11). It commands us not to let sin reign in our mortal body (verse 12). It forbids us to yield our members to the service of sin (verse 13). Chapter 7 explains that the law has no power to enable anyone to obey such commands and that indwelling sin prevents all Christians from carrying out these commands perfectly or even consistently. In chapter 8 Paul explains what accounts for the fact that we are able to obey such directives to any extent. Despite the influence which indwelling sin brings to bear upon us, we really do delight in God's will (7:22), and we really are serving the law of God (7:25). By what power do we reckon, yield, delight, and serve?

Remember, in all of our spiritual achievements we do nothing perfectly.

THE BELIEVER'S SANCTIFICATION
(Romans 8:1-13)

The question of our condemnation is settled. We have freedom from the guilt and penalty of sin (verse 1). Paul is still in the process of explaining why justified people cannot continue in slavery to the dictates of indwelling sin. Justification does not free anyone from the rule and reign of sin. Nor does it place any power in us which makes us behave in a godly manner. Moreover, regeneration of itself does not equip us to prevail over the onslaughts of the flesh nature. In regeneration we receive the life of God, but that in itself does not fit us for the fight any more than being born into this world makes a soldier prepared for battle. We need something more than justification, reconciliation, or regeneration; we need enabling power. And for this reason the Holy Spirit of power has taken up His permanent residence in every Christian. It is He who restrains the power of indwelling sin and puts godly dispositions into the soul. The gracious influences of the indwelling Spirit prevail against the influences of indwelling

Regeneration is that act of the Holy Spirit whereby He makes alive the dead human spirit by communicating to it a divine principle of life. It is a supernatural quickening from spiritual death (Ephesians 2:5). To be spiritually dead means to be alienated from

the life of God
and destitute of
the Spirit of God.
A regenerate
person is alive
unto God and is
a new creature.

sin, and for this reason we are free from slavery to sin and exempt from the consequences such enslavement involves—namely, eternal death (verse 2).

The authority of the law was no match for indwelling sin. The law was powerless in the face of such corruption. But God dealt effectively with sin by sending His own Son to do combat with it. The battlefield was the sinless human nature of Christ (verse 3). Here the battle was fought and won. The victory secured, He gave sin a suspended sentence but stripped it of its sovereign power. The final execution of sin awaits our glorification. At that time, sin will be forever banished from us. Meanwhile, the Holy Spirit has undertaken the ministry of preventing indwelling sin from regaining its former dominion.

Christ was
"separate from
sinners"
(Hebrews 7:26);
"without sin"
(Hebrews 4:15);
solicitation to sin
found nothing in
Him which had
any affinity with
sin (John 14:30).
He had no
corrupt principle
in Him.
Indwelling sin
did not exist in
His humanity.

The negative ministry of restraint, however, would not produce positive righteousness in us, and so the Holy Spirit works to produce His own holy characteristics in us. This accounts for the fact that we spontaneously fulfill the righteous requirements of the law even though we might not know what it commands (verse 4). The predominant inclination of our whole being is to follow the Holy Spirit, and it is the Spirit's powerful ministry which inclines our disposition in this direction.

People who are not indwelt by the Spirit are moving in just the opposite direction. The prevailing bent of their minds is toward those things which cater to their inborn depravity (verse 5). They are totally controlled by the flesh nature because this is the only nature they possess. Those who are indwelt by the Spirit, however, are so controlled by the Spirit that it is their general tendency to become more and more engrossed in the things of the Spirit. The mind of the unsaved man is totally under the domination of inborn sin. His mind is in a state of spiritual death, making it impossible for him to have one godly thought (verse 6). The mind of the Christian is receiving holy impulses from the indwelling Spirit of life, making external life and peace a reality in his thoughts and experience.

The mind of the unsaved man, controlled as it is by his inward corruption, has no delight in God or His law. Any thought of performing the will of God is foreign to him, for his life is ego-centric rather than theo-centric. His ultimate goal in life is to derive as much personal satisfaction as possible. He is not concerned with the theological maxim which teaches that the chief end of man is to glorify God. As a matter of fact, unless he receives a brand-new life through faith in Jesus Christ, he will never submit to God's law. Indeed, it is utterly impossible for him to submit to the law of God until the chains of slavery to sin are broken (verse 7). And, as long as his mind, will, and emotions are dominated by sin, his life is unacceptable to God. Paul says categorically, "So then they that are in the flesh cannot please God" (verse 8).

That is a depressing but factual picture of the condition of every unsaved person. The situation of the Christian is very different indeed. He is not "in the flesh" and, therefore, not controlled by the flesh nature. The Holy Spirit lives in him to make certain that his mind, emotions, and will never come under the tyranny of sin again. This unique experience of the Christian, however, does not make him different from the unsaved man so far as the power of death working in his physical body is concerned. The indwelling Spirit has not

Note that the natural man—the unregenerate person— "receiveth not the things of the Spirit... neither can he know them" (I Corinthians 2:14).

The word "law" in Romans does not always mean Mosaic law. Here it refers to the revealed will of God.

reversed the process of death in us yet; we are mortal because of sin (verse 10).

But our bodies have a different future from that of the unsaved. Our bodies are going to be raised and glorified, and the Spirit's residence within is our guarantee of eventual liberation from physical death (verse 11). To follow the dictates of indwelling sin as a habit of life, then, is a contradiction to everything our present liberation implies (verse 12). In fact, such a bent of mind is certain evidence of an unregenerate state which issues in eternal death. But if we are mortifying the flesh, we can be sure the reason is that the indwelling Spirit is prompting it. This is an evidence of a regenerate state which issues in eternal life (verse 13).

THE BELIEVER'S SONSHIP
(Romans 8:14-25)

How do you explain the fact that Christians obey the commands to reckon themselves dead to sin, yield themselves to God, and walk in the Spirit? There is only one adequate explanation: the indwelling Spirit leads us to do these things (verse 14). All of the sons of God are Spirit-led; therefore, all of the sons of God are obeying these commands—not perfectly, of course, but to the degree that He enables. There is no such creature as a Christian who is not being led by the Spirit. By definition, a Christian is a person who is being led by the Spirit to mortify indwelling sin. This is one of the reasons that no Christian can continue under the dominion of sin.

The Christian is not a servant of sin but a son of the heavenly Father. But if it were not for the indwelling Spirit, we would be too feeble to utter the faintest cry to the Father (verse 15). In fact, we would not know that we had come into the status of sonship if the Spirit within were not registering this fact upon our consciousness (verse 16). And then, of course, when we begin to see the outward effects that result from the Spirit's gracious operation in our souls, we have further confirmation that we really are God's children. Then it comes to us with new appreciation that since we are God's children, we must be His heirs (verse 17).

If suffering still besets us, let's not conclude that we are not God's children. Rather, it is a further proof that we are His own, and He is preparing us for glory by means of privations and perils in this life. We shall share Christ's glory; shall we not participate in His sufferings first? To say that the suffering cannot be compared with the glory is the understatement of all time (verse 18).

It is true that as heirs we shall receive all of the possessions of the Father. It is also true that God Himself is the inheritance of His people (Genesis 15:1; Numbers 18:20).

Christians have something in common with creation around them. Both are temporarily groaning under the power of corruption, and both are eagerly anticipating the final deliverance (verse 19). Creation will not attain the goal of its original design until the sons of God reach the final stage of their sanctification—the stage of glory. Our manifestation includes the eradication of every reminder of our present corruption, when we shall be transformed into the perfect image of Jesus Christ—spirit, soul, and body.

"As we have borne the image of the earthy, we shall also bear the image of the heavenly" (I Corinthians 15:49).

That brings up the subject of what happened to creation in order to reduce it to its present state of degradation and disorganization. Verse 20 strongly implies that creation is not now in the state in which it was originally created. Creation is "not willingly" thwarted from reaching its proper end.

In many instances it is man's carelessness and greed that turn lands into deserts and wildernesses. Man's selfishness is more and more upsetting the ecological balance in nature. All forms of life suffer from man's misuse and abuse of nature.

Jesus referred to the glorification of nature as a "regeneration" (Matthew 19:28).

As in the Christian, a law works in creation to hinder it from attaining perfection. Scientists call it the second law of thermodynamics. When Adam sinned, this law began to operate in nature with the result that all things tend toward decay and death—including the human body. Add to this man's sinful abuse of the resources of nature, and you can understand why the natural world is as it is.

The present order will not continue indefinitely. Creation will undergo a regeneration in which it will be freed from the second law of thermodynamics (verse 21). We need not expect an annihilation of the present order. It is more likely to be a transformation. The whole material universe will be uplifted into the sphere of spirit. The omnipotence of the Holy Spirit will effect the glorification of earth just as surely as He will glorify our mortal and corruptible bodies. The result of one will be a spiritual universe; the result of the other will be a spiritual body. The new estate of nature will match man's estate in glory.

Presently, birthpangs have seized upon nature; it agonizes like a woman in travail. All of its intricate and minute parts feel the anguish (verse 22). How similar is the Christian's present agony over the stirrings of indwelling sin. How we long to be delivered of this dead weight! This is the reason that we look forward so earnestly to the final stage of our adoption—the redemption of the body (verse 23). The indwelling Spirit is the earnest of the promised liberty and glory. The fact that we groan in grief over the assaults of indwelling sin is proof that the Spirit indwells us. The Spirit within is creating in us such a loathing for our sin that we thus agonize.

The great consolation is our hope of full salvation (verse 24). We have been saved from the penalty of sin, we are being saved from the power of sin, and we shall be saved from the presence of sin. In this joyous prospect of final victory we live. This hope is the incentive we need for persevering to the very end (verse 25). Our constancy in the things of the Spirit depends upon this hope, and for that reason the Holy Spirit keeps the blessed hope burning in our hearts.

FOOD FOR THOUGHT

"All that has been done by God the Father and by God the Son must be ineffectual to us, unless the Spirit shall reveal those things to our souls."

—Charles Haddon Spurgeon

NOW TEST YOUR KNOWLEDGE

Underline the correct answer:

1. Justification frees us from the power, presence, penalty of sin.

2. Sanctification frees us from the power, presence, penalty of sin.

3. Glorification frees us from the power, presence, penalty of sin.

4. By regeneration we receive power to overcome, life from God, sonship.

5. Adoption has to do with children, sons, servants.

6. The will of the unsaved man is neutral, free, enslaved.

7. The leading of the Spirit refers to His control, His providential guidance, His indwelling presence.

8. God's ultimate goal for nature is glorification, annihilation, degeneration.

9. The indwelling Spirit removes, restrains, rebukes indwelling sin in all believers.

10. Indwelling sin is the cause of the Christian's gladness, growth, groaning.

YOU ARE ETERNALLY SECURE

8

LESSON SCRIPTURE
Romans 8:26—9:33

RELATED SCRIPTURE
Ephesians 1:1-14;
II Thessalonians 2:13-17;
II Timothy 1:9; Titus 3:5; I Peter 1:2

LESSON AIM
To find in God's eternal purpose the
only sufficient basis for the Chris-
tian's eternal security; to see how
Israel's present unbelief relates to
God's eternal purpose.

LEARN BY HEART
"And we know that all things work
together for good to them that love
God, to them who are the called according to his purpose" (Romans
8:28).

EVERY DAY WITH THE WORD

Monday	Chosen seed	Deuteronomy 4:31-40
Tuesday	Chosen people	Deuteronomy 7:6-11
Wednesday	Chosen king	Deuteronomy 17:14-20
Thursday	Chosen priests	Deuteronomy 18:1-8
Friday	Chosen tribe	Psalm 78:65-72
Saturday	Chosen apostles	Luke 6:12-19
Sunday	Chosen vessel	Acts 9:10-16

STUDENT'S NOTEBOOK

This column is for
the student who
desires additional
study of the lesson
theme.

LESSON PREPARATION

The certainty of the Christian's full and final
salvation rests upon manifold assurances. We
have been acquitted of guilt (Romans 8:1). We

Can you find any other foundations for the believer's security besides those listed here? Don't neglect John 10 in this connection.

have been freed from sin's dominion (verse 2). The Holy Spirit is enabling us to meet God's standard of righteousness (verse 4). We are neither in the flesh nor walking after the flesh (verses 5,9). We are sons of God and, therefore, under Spirit-control (verse 14). We are hopefully and patiently awaiting deliverance from our natural corruption (verses 23-25). Our salvation does not depend upon human failure; it depends ultimately upon the sovereign purpose of God. God cannot fail. This truth gives us the most assurance.

GOD'S SOVEREIGN PURPOSE TOWARD THE CHRISTIAN
(Romans 8:26-39)

Persevering and prevailing prayer is essential to the Christian life. Thanks be to God, no true Christian can fail in the exercise of effectual prayer because the indwelling Spirit causes us to pray. More than that, He instructs us in the topics which we should make a matter of prayer (verse 26). Although we are regenerate persons, we are still so ignorant and illiterate when it comes to prayer that if it were not for the intercession of the Spirit, we would not be able to say anything fit for God's holy ears. The Spirit interprets our deepest needs and intelligently presents them to the Father (verse 27). The fact that we are full of frailties is no barrier to our engaging in effectual prayer.

The first time we see Saul of Tarsus after his conversion, he is praying. Prayer is to the Christian what breathing is to a newborn baby. See Acts 9:11.

All of the things that cause us to groan in prayer—natural weaknesses, adversities, the assaults of Satan, the uprisings of indwelling sin—are contributing to our progress in sanctification. God is working *everything* together for the good of the Christian (verse 28). Even our failures are part of God's gracious purpose to make us

Poor old Jacob thought that everything was working against him, and all the while the adversities were more and more Christlike. This applies only to the Christian. All things are working together to bring the non-Christian to ruin.

God's promise to bring the Christian safely to Heaven and glory cannot fail, for God has resolutely purposed to do so. In accordance with His own purpose, He foreknew us (verse 29). This means that He determined from eternity to choose and love us, not because of any virtue in us but because this was part of His plan. In harmony with that same determinate purpose, God predestinated us to be conformed to Christ. This means that God purposed to bring us to the ultimate destination to which he had appointed us from eternity. It included our getting to be more like Christ every day and finally receiving a body like His glorious body. We are eternally secure because foreknowledge has determined the outcome and predestination is bringing it to pass.

Part of what God purposed to do from eternity is already history. At one moment in the past he called us and we responded in faith to the divine voice (verse 30). Through our response of faith God justified us. Both the calling and the justification were assured from eternity. Our glorification is just as certain to come to pass as was our calling and justification. It cannot fail, for nothing can thwart God's determinate purpose.

In delivering up His only Son, God gave us a guarantee that because He brought to pass the greater (our justification), He will have no difficulty in accomplishing the lesser (our glorification). Our justification has been secured by the death of Christ (verse 33), and our ultimate sanctification is assured by the resurrection and intercession of Christ (verse 34).

really part of God's plan to preserve him and all of his sons (Genesis 42:36). The events of the book of Esther are another case in point.

Note that God's plan for the Christian reaches from eternity to eternity.

"For the Lord of hosts hath purposed, and who shall disannul it?" (Isaiah 14:27).

We are so secure in the love of Christ that nothing can detach us from His powerful embrace. The "nothing" includes everything and anything you can think of: the severest trials imaginable (verses 35-37), the highest orders of angelic beings, the power of death, all that we encounter in life, the relationships of time (verse 38), the dimensions of space, and whatever other category or creature comes to mind (verse 39). We never get by by the skin of our teeth; rather, we triumph magnificently over all foes through the strength Christ gives.

In verse 35 Paul is talking about Christ's love for us, not our love for Christ. 'We love Him because He first loved us" (I John 4:19).

Philippians 4:13

GOD'S SOVEREIGN PURPOSE TOWARD ISRAEL
(Romans 9:1-33)

God's purpose for Israel resembles in some respects His purpose for the Christian. He foreknew Israel, set His love upon her, gave the nation the privilege of sonship, held out to her unconditional promises, and appointed her to fulfill a grand role in redemptive history. But Israel has not come to the appointed destiny. Has the determinate purpose of God failed? If the soverign purpose of God can be thwarted by Israel's failure, then His sovereign purpose can also be thwarted by the Christian's failure. Romans 9—11 deals with this thorny problem.

The national unbelief of Israel is a fact to be reckoned with. They officially rejected their Messiah. Every thought of it brought Paul intense pain (verses 1,2). He would gladly have forfeited his own salvation if that were possible and if it would bring Israel to faith in Christ (verse 3). Israel's unique advantages left her with no excuse

Individual Israelites were not sons. The whole nation was a son (Hosea 11:1). God adopted the nation from among the other nations and called them His own.

Israel's conduct on the day of the triumphal entry of Christ to the city of Jerusalem sealed their decision (Luke 19:42,44).

for crucifying her Messiah-God. The nation as a whole had enjoyed a relationship to God as His adopted son (verse 4). His glorious presence had resided among them in the Tabernacle and the Temple. He had entered into covenant arrangements with them. They alone of the people of earth had the written law of God, the sanctuary service, and the unconditional promises. They had descended from the patriarchs and were the race who gave birth to the Messiah (verse 5).

A covenant is not a mutual agreement. It is a relationship into which God enters with His people.

Israel's rejection of Christ has not thwarted God's determinate purpose. The rejection by the masses of Jewry was part of the eternal purpose and contributes to a larger purpose, as we shall see. God's gracious purpose did not apply to all of the natural descendants of Abraham; they applied only to a much smaller segment of the nation (verse 6). God's covenant-promises apply only to a select group of the children of Abraham. God cut Ishmael and his descendants off from being a recipient of these promises and chose Isaac and his descendants (verses 7-9). God counted only Isaac and his descendants as the true seed of Abraham.

Romans 11 deals with this matter at length.

As far as God was concerned, Isaac was Abraham's "only son" (Genesis 22:2).

God also discriminated between the sons of Isaac. Not all of the descendants of Isaac were the true seed of Abraham. God excluded Esau, the firstborn, and chose Jacob to be the heir of the promises to Abraham. Natural generation never entitled anyone to the promises. The decisive factor was always the sovereign choice of God. And we must not imagine that the divine choice was influenced by anything in the one whom God chose. A man's circumstances, character, morals, or works have no bearing upon God's choice, as the case of Jacob plainly shows. God's choice of Jacob illustrates the truth that God carries out His

Mathew 3:9; John 1:13

predetermined purpose through sovereign election (verse 11). For this reason God's purpose cannot fail no matter how much men fail.

God reversed the natural order or priority by causing the firstborn, Esau, to serve his younger brother Jacob (verse 12). He also made Jacob the object of His redeeming love and made Esau the object of His disfavor and displeasure (verse 13). These two divine actions will strike some people as evidence that God is unrighteous (verse 14). Paul reminds such objectors of two episodes from Israel's history which prove that God has a right to pardon whomever He pleases and punish whomever He pleases. Israel deserved His wrath for making a golden calf and for worshiping it (Exodus 32:1-10). They were unregenerate sinners, and yet God acted in mercy toward them just because He willed to show them mercy (verse 15). The will of man and the greatest exertions of man do not influence God to show mercy (verse 16).

Pharaoh was also an unregenerate sinner. Spiritually and morally, he was no worse or better than Israel, and yet God willed not to show him mercy. He chose, instead, to visit Pharaoh with His wrath and thus give Pharaoh the punishment which his insolence and stubbornness deserved (verses 17,18). Without knowing it, Pharaoh served God's predetermined purpose. God purposed that Israel should have an exhibition of His retributive justice and also of His mighty power. He chose to use the stubbornness of Pharaoh as the occasion to demonstrate both. The hardness of Pharaoh's heart was absolutely indispensable to the fulfillment of God's purpose to deliver Israel from Egypt by an act of omnipotence and despite the opposition of a world-power. God had the

---

Let us not tone down the fact that God hated Esau. There is a sense in which God hates the wicked (Psalm 5:5). As we progress in sanctification, we more and more hate what God hates. (Note Hebrews 1:9).

God did not cause Pharaoh to be wicked. God is not the author of sin. As an unregnerate man, Pharaoh was naturally full of evil.

God used Pharaoh's innate wickedness to serve His purpose.

power to make Pharaoh's hard heart soft, but this would not have fulfilled the purpose which he had planned for Israel. God was working all things together for His chosen people.

If the stubbornness of Pharaoh contributed to God's determinate purpose, how can anyone blame Pharaoh? Wasn't he just a victim of God's irresistible decree (verse 19)? Such questions only reveal the ignorance of men; they also indicate how eager men always are to shift all responsibility upon God and thus justify their wickedness. Pharaoh got exactly what he deserved.

But what right has any man to cross-examine the Creator for His actions (verse 20)? Certainly you don't expect that a piece of pottery will dictate to the potter what purpose it will serve. The will of the potter determines whether the vessel will serve honorable or dishonorable uses (verse 21). In like manner, God's will determines whether a man, like Pharaoh, will serve to exhibit His patient endurance of sinners and finally His wrath against them (verse 22): or whether, like Israel, a man will become an exhibition of God's pardoning mercy and eventually a participant in the glory for which God prepared him (verse 23).

Moreover, if God wills to show the Gentiles mercy (verse 24), that, too, is perfectly compatible with what the Old Testament predicted He would do (verse 25,26). Meanwhile, if God wills not to show mercy to the mass of Jewry, this is no more than what the Old Testament anticipated (verses 27,28). God has His own purpose for abandoning Israel to hardness of heart. Israel's present state of apostasy from God is no evidence that human failure can thwart God's purpose; for God, in His eternal purpose, intended to save only a remnant

Sidenotes:

Consider how many times Pharaoh hardened his own heart before we read that God hardened it.

Romans 9:23 specifically says that God prepares the vessels of mercy unto glory. Verse 22 does not say that God fits the vessels of wrath to destruction.

In Romans 11 we shall learn that the present condition of Jewry is only temporary.

of Israel during the church age (verse 29). Every Jew who comes to Christ is proof of the changelessness of God's purpose.

In God's purpose masses of Gentiles are now receiving imputed righteousness by faith in Christ (verse 30). These Gentiles are the spiritual seed of Abraham and spiritual heirs of the promises. God's word to Abraham is being partially fulfilled through the conversion of Gentiles now. Meanwhile, masses of Jews are not receiving imputed righteousness. They foolishly imagine that they can attain righteousness through human effort (verse 31). They continue to reject their Messiah (verse 32). Their minds are beclouded with unbelief, and so they feel only repugnance for a blood atonement that involves a crucified Messiah (verse 33). With respect to these unbelieving Jews, the divine purpose has not failed. They are not the true seed of Abraham in the first place and, therefore, have no claim on the covenant promise. Besides that, God is using the unbelief of Israel as His means of fulfilling His predetermined purpose for the Gentiles. This will become more clear in Romans 10—11.

FOOD FOR THOUGHT

"The purposes of God are sometimes delayed but never abandoned."

—Selected

NOW TEST YOUR KNOWLEDGE

Answer true or false:

1. Everything that comes to pass is good.
2. God is working all things together for the sinner's good.
3. Foreknowledge is nothing more than foresight.
4. Some things come to pass which take God by surprise.
5. Some things come to pass which are not a part of God's overall purpose.
6. God causes some people to sin so that He can use their sin to accomplish a higher purpose.
7. Some things which God purposes to come to pass will never come to pass.
8. Human failure is a decisive factor in whether God's purpose comes to pass.
9. God chose Jacob because He foresaw that Jacob would be a righteous man.
10. The present unbelief of Israel proves that God cannot carry out all of His predetermined purposes.
11. Pharaoh did not deserve the punishment which he received from God; he was just a victim of God's irresistible will.
12. God has the sole right to decide what use He will make of His creatures.
13. None of the promises which God gave to Abraham are being fulfilled in any sense today.
14. It is possible to be a true Christian and yet never pray.
15. The new birth is what makes our prayers well-pleasing to God.

GOD KEEPS HIS PROMISES

9

LESSON SCRIPTURE
Romans 10:1—11:36

RELATED SCRIPTURE
Jeremiah 31:31-40; 32:36—33:26;
Ezekiel 36:16-38; Amos 9:11-15;
Acts 15:13-18

LESSON AIM
To discover how many of the
Abrahamic promises are being
fulfilled to Jews and Gentiles today;
to determine which promises remain
yet to be fulfilled, to whom they will
be fulfilled, and when they will be
fulfilled.

LEARN BY HEART
"For I would not, brethren, that ye
should be ignorant of this mystery,
lest ye should be wise in your own
conceits; that blindness in part is
happened to Israel, until the fulness
of the Gentiles be come in"
(Romans 11:25).

STUDENT'S NOTEBOOK

This column is for
the student who
desires additional
study of the lesson
theme.

EVERY DAY WITH THE WORD

Monday	Covenant with Noah	Genesis 9:1-17
Tuesday	Covenant with Abraham	Genesis 15:1-21
Wednesday	Covenant with Isaac	Genesis 26:1-5,24,25
Thursday	Covenant with Jacob	Genesis 28:10-22
Friday	Covenant with Israel	Exodus 19:1-13
Saturday	Covenant with the Land	Deuteronomy 29:1-8
Sunday	Covenant with David	II Samuel 7:4-17

LESSON PREPARATION

| Think of a train speeding on its way. Suddenly

it grinds to a halt and then moves slowly forward. The passengers become aware of the fact that it is being placed on a siding. In a few minutes an express roars through on the main line. When the express has passed, the train pulls out from its siding, approaches the main track, and continues to its destination.

During the church age, Israel stands still on the siding while God is calling out Jews and Gentiles to complete the church. When His purpose for the church is fulfilled, Israel will resume her progress in the plan of God.

Acts 15:14-17

THE REJECTION OF ISRAEL
(Romans 10:1-21)

The main issue in Romans 9—11 is whether God's purpose toward Israel has failed. Have the promises which God gave to Abraham and his seed come to nothing? At the moment, Israel as a nation has not become a recipient of the blessings of salvation which God promised Abraham's heirs. They remain unbelieving and unsaved (verse 1). The reason the Jewish nation is lost is that they are aiming their religious enthusiasm in the wrong direction (verse 2). They are willfully ignorant of the perfect righteousness with which God clothes sinners, and so they are fervently engaged in pursuing a legal righteousness by means of scrupulous attention to the law of Moses (verse 3).

Galatians 3:6-9 assures us that God's promise to Abraham with regard to his heirs involves personal salvation and includes Gentiles who believe as Abraham believed.

The Jews are lost because they refuse to admit that no one can attain the divine standard by human effort. They deny that Jesus Christ perfectly fulfilled the righteous requirements of the law and that the law of Moses reached its terminal point in Christ (verse 4). It is quite true that

Saul of Tarsus had the same

kind of zeal which the Jews manifested. In the eyes of men he was blameless. But he came to realize that an earned righteousness was inadequate, and so he abandoned his futile efforts at lawkeeping and received the righteousness of Christ (Philippians 3:6-9).

the Mosaic law offered a righteousness by means of observances, but in order for anyone to attain it, he had to conform to the law perfectly and permanently (verse 5).

Human effort cannot achieve righteousness. No man can ascend into Heaven or descend into Hades to obtain it (verses 6,7). Such attempts amount to saying either that Christ did not become the incarnate Son, did not die, did not rise from the dead, and did not return to the Father or that His work was incomplete and that human endeavors must supplement what He did. The preaching and teaching of God's servants have explained the way of righteousness. It is as near as the sound of the truth. Nothing remains except for men to believe what they hear (verse 8). They must believe that God raised the Lord Jesus from the dead. This presupposes that they believe He died to justify them freely and that He arose to confirm His right and power to save them (verse 9). In order to receive a divine righteousness, they must have the kind of faith which openly confesses that Jesus is Lord.

God's way of righteousness is accessible to all. Faith is the condition for receiving it, and all who believe will never be disappointed with the results (verse 11). Jews need faith in Christ equally as much as Gentiles (verse 12). Salvation does not depend upon a man's racial connections, religious privileges, or ecclesiastical zeal; it depends upon whether he will call upon the Lord Jesus Christ to save him (verse 13). Calling upon Christ takes for granted that a man believes the claims of Christ. He cannot believe, however, until he has heard. He cannot hear unless someone explains the truth. The explanation of the truth depends upon the

To call upon the name of the Lord means to worship Him, exercise a reliance upon Him, believe Him, coming of a preacher or teacher of the truth who has been sent to declare it (verses 14,15).

The reason Jewish unbelief is inexcusable is that God sent her preachers of the gospel, and Israel refused to believe the message which promised an imputed righteousness by faith in Christ (verse 16). If Israel had not heard the Word of truth, we might make some allowances for her lack of faith (verse 17); but she did hear, and so she is more blameworthy for rejecting it. In fact, Jews were the first to hear it. Wherever Jews resided, the first-century messengers took them the good news (verse 18). But Jewish guilt goes still deeper, for they were well aware that the Gentiles were enjoying the blessings of righteousness which Jews had striven for and failed to attain (verses 19,20). Whenever Gentiles received the promises by faith, Jews became furious with those who offered Gentiles a full and free salvation.

Jewish unbelief is even more wicked in light of the fact that for centuries God made them overtures of mercy and pardon which they ignored. They continued to be stubborn, proud, and disobedient, just as Isaiah had predicted (verse 21). Jewish unbelief did not take God by surprise; it did not frustrate His predeterminate purpose. Rather, the attitude of the Jews played a significant role in the working out of His purpose for Gentiles. Nevertheless, the full responsibility of Jewish unbelief lies on their own doorstep.

and trust him. The first reference to this is Genesis 4:26. More is involved than just a prayer.

It was Paul's strategy to head first to the Jewish synagogue and give the Jews the first opportunity to hear. As soon as they repudiated the message, he turned his attention to the Gentiles.

THE RESTORATION OF ISRAEL
(Romans 11:1-36)

We come back again to the question, "Has Jewish unbelief annulled God's covenant promise

It may be that his parents named him after King Saul. Saul was a giant physically but a midget spiritually. His namesake was a giant spiritually.

Remember, Abraham's true heirs do not include all of his descendants or only his physical descendants. They do include all righteous Jews and all righteous Gentiles.

Most predicted the terrible consequences of Israel remaining in apostasy (Deuteronomy 28:15-68). He also

to Abraham and thus brought the divine purpose to failure?'' Certainly not! The conversion of Saul of Tarsus, a descendant of the tribe of Benjamin, proves that the setting aside of Israel is not total (verse 1). Paul had become a recipient of the spiritual blessings promised to Abraham's seed.

The present apostasy of Israel as a nation resembles the period of Elijah when he imagined he was the only faithful prophet left (verses 2,3). But just as God then preserved 7,000 godly Jews in the midst of national unbelief, so He now (during the church age) has a group of elect Jews who constitute a small remnant of believers amidst national unbelief (verse 5). These believing Jews are enjoying the spiritual blessings of salvation which God promised to Abraham's heirs. Nationally, Jews are not attaining the status of righteousness before God despite all of their fleshly efforts, but elect Jews whom God is adding to the church are attaining this status by faith (verse 7).

The continued hardness of the majority of Jews is a judgment upon the nation as a result of their turning a deaf ear to the preaching of the word in early apostolic times. Their present blindness is judicial (verse 8). Their extraordinary privileges and unique heritage are today a snare to them, for they have become preoccupied with the outward symbols of salvation rather than with salvation itself (verse 9). The consequences are terrible; they are reduced to a servile condition (verse 10).

Individual Jews here and there are trusting Christ, but what about Israel as a whole? Has the nation fallen never to rise again (verse 11)? Perish the thought! The present unbelief of Jewry is part of God's purpose to bring the Gentiles into the experience of the Abrahamic blessings. God has overruled the apostasy of Jews by bringing salvation to the Gentiles. But God has not lost sight of His long-range plans for national Israel. The entire Bible anticipates a time when Jews as a whole will enjoy the Abrahamic promises. The present reduction of the true Israel to a small number of believing Jews is only a pledge of a later full-scale conversion of the whole nation (verse 12).

predicted their final restoration (Deuteronomy 29:1-15; 30:1-20).

Paul understood God's plan of casting national Israel aside for the duration of the church age, and he recognized that his own special ministry concerned the Gentiles, but these factors did not stop him from earnestly trying to win Jews to Christ (verses 13,14). He also knew that his ministry among the Gentiles, as successful as it would be, would never reach the dimensions during the church age that it would reach in the millennial age when national Israel would be regenerated and restored to God's favor. Not until Jews are converted to Christ on a national scale will God do His greatest work among the Gentiles (verse 15).

Their restoration depends upon Israel's repentance and faith, and God will give them both of these graces.

The present firstfruits among both Jews and Gentiles guarantee that the rest of the harvest of salvation will follow (verse 16). For the present, however, God has cut national Israel off from being recipients of the Abrahamic promises, and He has introduced Gentiles to these rich promises (verse 17). Gentiles should remember, however, that Gentile inclusion is the result of God's grace and not their merit. They are no better than the unbelieving Jews, and they are not stronger to stand. They stand by faith, and so they have no ground for glorying in what they are by nature (verse 18-20).

Gentiles are enjoying the spiritual promises but not the national promises to Abraham.

Gentiles who do not persevere in spiritual things prove thereby that they were never truly

The emphasis in Romans 11

concerns Jews and Gentiles, not the church.

The Gentile nations will be demoted from their present political ascendancy to make room for the political supremacy of Israel in the millennium. During the times of the Gentiles, the Gentiles will prove themselves utterly unworthy of their God-given privileges.

regenerate, and they will be cut off from their opportunities just as the unbelieving Jews were (verses 21,22). On the other hand, if Jews on a national scale believe, God will restore them to favor and Abrahamic blessings (verse 23). It is far less difficult to engraft Israel to the natural stock of Abrahamic promises than to engraft Gentiles, who are not Abraham's physical descendants in the first place (verse 24).

The present unbelief of national Israel, therefore, is neither total nor permanent. When God has completed His special work of calling out of the Gentiles a people for His name, then He will resume His special dealings with Israel as a nation (verse 25). After the rapture of the church, God will raise up a group of 144,000 believing Jews who will turn other Jews (and Gentiles, too, for that matter) to righteousness. These Jews will constitute a future remnant, many of whom will survive the tribulation judgments. They will be finally delivered from their enemies by the return of Christ (verse 26).

These Jews will be the charter members of the millennial kingdom. To these Jews God will fulfill in full the promises of the Abrahamic, the Palestinian, The Davidic, and the New covenants. They will enjoy the spiritual blessings of righteousness, reconciliation, regeneration, and remission of sin (verse 27). They will also receive the national promises, which include reunion of the tribes, repatriation to the land of Israel, reorganization of the Davidic government, reconstruction of Israel's cities, and the reinstitution of the ceremonial rites in the rebuilt Temple. All of these events are guaranteed by God's love for Abraham, Isaac, and Jacob (verse 28) and by the unchangeableness of His purpose (verse 29).

The covenants into which God entered with Abraham and his seed and with King David and his dynasty are irrevocable covenants. Human failure may temporarily delay the fulfillment of these covenants, for God will not fulfill the promises which these covenants guarantee until Israel as a whole deposits faith in the Lord Jesus Christ as her Messiah and Lord. Israel has not yet met the condition of faith, but this will not ultimately thwart God's purpose for the simple reason that God intends to reverse their present hardness and unbelief by giving them a heart to perceive and eyes to see and ears to hear (Deuteronomy 29:4).

For more information on the content of these covenants, see Accent-B/P's course *Clarifying God's Covenants.*

The whole scheme is God's wise design to dispense His mercy on a universal scale (verses 30-32). He has been pursuing this plan from age to age, and no act of human rebellion can ultimately thwart His purpose. He will reach His predetermined goal by methods which would never occur to finite minds and which cause us to exclaim in worshipful praise (verses 33-36).

FOOD FOR THOUGHT

"Go, then, and bend your knee to pray for Israel's ancient race;
Ask the dear Saviour every day to call them by His grace.
Go, for a debt of love is due from Christian Gentiles to the Jew."

—Unknown

Underscore the correct answer.

1. The present blindness of Israel is the fault of the Jews, the Gentiles, the Lord.

2. In order to attain righteousness through lawkeeping, a man had to keep the law perfectly, as well as he could, during special religious seasons.

3. Israel is not saved because the nation lacked the opportunity, because God blinded her, because she refused to believe.

4. Saved Jews are now enjoying the temporal, spiritual, material blessings which God promised to Abraham's righteous heirs.

5. During the millennial age Jews will enjoy only material blessings, only spiritual blessings, both material and spiritual blessings.

6. God's purpose for national Israel has been cancelled, delayed, defeated through Jewish unbelief.

7. The only time in history when the majority of Jews are righteous is the Mosaic age, the church age, the tribulation period, the millennial age.

8. The greatest number of Gentiles will be righteous during the church age, the tribulation period, the millennial age.

9. God's covenants are irreconcilable, irrevocable, irrational.

10. The main requirements for receiving the Abrahamic promises is faith, race, religious privilege.

YOU ARE BEING TRANSFORMED

LESSON SCRIPTURE
Romans 12:1—13:7

RELATED SCRIPTURE
Matthew 5—7; I Corinthians 12—13;
Ephesians 4—6; I Peter 2:13-17.

LESSON AIM
To fulfill our duty toward God,
ourselves, other Christians,
neighbors, enemies, government,
and Christian service.

LEARN BY HEART
"I beseech you therefore, brethren,
by the mercies of God, that ye present your bodies a living sacrifice,
holy, acceptable unto God, which is
your reasonable service" (Romans
12:1).

EVERY DAY WITH THE WORD

Monday	Grace to believe	Acts 18:24-28
Tuesday	Grace to build	I Corinthians 3:5-11
Wednesday	Grace to behave	II Corinthians 1:8-14
Thursday	Grace to give	II Corinthians 8:7-15
Friday	Grace to glory	II Corinthians 12:1-10
Saturday	Grace to go	Galatians 2:1-10
Sunday	Grace to grow	II Peter 3:10-18

STUDENT'S NOTEBOOK

This column is for
the student who
desires additional
study of the lesson
theme.

LESSON PREPARATION

Thus far in the epistle to the Romans, the Holy
Spirit has brought colossal truths before us—sin,
condemnation, atonement, justification, sanctification, identification with Christ in His death,

burial, and resurrection. We have learned about God's past, present, and future dealings with Israel. Upon this doctrinal foundation, the Apostle Paul now builds the superstructure of the Christian life. Ethics without solid doctrinal content is nothing more than empty moralizing. Apart from the believer's vital union with Christ, Christian behavior would be impossible. The Christian life is the practical outworking of the fact that we are no longer under the dominion of sin. The Christian life is the transformed and sanctified life, and the final section in the book of Romans concentrates on this fact.

ETHICAL RELATIONSHIPS INSIDE THE FAMILY
(Romans 12:1-16)

If sanctification does not embrace the physical body, then it is only an impractical and theoretical doctrine. The sanctifying ministry of the Spirit includes the spirit, the soul, *and the body* (I Thessalonians 5:23). It is the body which gives expression to our inward impulses, and so it is essential that this instrument come under the control of the Spirit. For this reason Paul urges Christians to put their bodies at God's disposal (verse 1). It is as necessary to Christian growth and service as it is a reasonable and holy consecration.

Nothing is a greater hindrance to the sanctification of our bodies than the influences of the space age. Modern fashions do very little for fostering personal modesty and purity. Current thinking tends to shape our attitudes toward hemlines, haircuts, habits, homes, and health—indeed, toward virtually every aspect of life. But it contributes nothing to sanctification. Sanctification of the body is the result of the inward work of the Holy Spirit on the mind (verse 2). By His grace He changes our attitudes toward the moral climate of our generation, and this transformation of our minds has its effects upon the way we dress and the use to which we put our bodies. When the Holy Spirit adjusts our minds, emotions, and wills to the Word of God, we are able to do what God considers "good, and acceptable, and perfect."

The Word of God is always the mirror of the will of God.

Speaking of the mind, we need to entertain a right opinion about ourselves in order to make progress in sanctification. When we begin to realize that we are what we are by the grace of God, then we perceive the nonsense of feeling proud of our gifts and graces (verse 3). By transforming and renewing our minds, the Holy Spirit enables us to evaluate ourselves for what we really are rather than for what we pretend to be. An honest opinion of ourselves will be a humble opinion. It will neither exaggerate our worth nor depreciate it.

We grow in a humble regard toward ourselves as we realize that we are all vital parts of a living organism—the body of Christ (verse 5). Each part has its own special function which promotes the health of the whole. God has set each one of us in the body exactly where He wants us. You are an eye, an ear, a hand, a foot, etc., by His sovereign appointment. He determined your place in the body according to His purpose, not according to your merits or talents. By grace you are what you are and function as you do (verse 6). Why, then, should you feel either conceited or cheated? And why would you rather be something other than

God appoints His servants to their respective roles

what God has made you? Why are you jealous over what God has given to someone else?

By the Spirit's illuminating power each one of us must decide what our supernatural endowment is and then by His grace give ourselves to exercising and cultivating it. The gifts vary: preaching, ministry, teaching, exhorting, giving, ruling, showing mercy (verses 6-8); but every gift is necessary to the edifying of a church and to the ongoing of the gospel. Find your place and fulfill your function.

Growth in sanctification means growth in genuine love (verse 9). Christians are responsible to abound in this virtue, and it is the inward influences of the Spirit at work on the affections which make love to increase. Christian love is a supernatural quality of affection that partakes of the nature of Christ's love for us. It is not an indulgent love but a love which feels an affinity for everything that is good and an abhorrence for everything that is evil.

The sanctifying ministry of the Spirit causes the believer to feel esteem for members of the Christian brotherhood (verse 10). It is the sort of admiration which prompts us to be the first to congratulate a brother for his contribution to God's work. We are eager for him to get the credit and quite content when we get no credit. The sanctifying influences of the Spirit touch every facet of our being. The Spirit can take a naturally lethargic person and fire him with spiritual enthusiasm (verse 11). Under the control of the Spirit, Christian zeal never becomes fanatical, Christian love is never selfish and lenient, and Christian devotion never centers on any other object except Christ Himself.

Progressive sanctification affects our hope by enabling us to "hope perfectly to the end." The Spirit turns our attention to the arrival of Jesus Christ and our future salvation. Our hope in Christ is the source of our present joy (verse 12); indeed, our gladness is nothing less than the joy of the Holy Ghost. It is hope that keeps us patient in affliction. Hope motivates us to persevere through fire and flood. Christian hope is never uncertain, Christian joy is never a giddy exhilaration, and Christian patience is never a fatal and Stoic resignation. We put on these virtues by spending time in the prayer closet.

Sanctification makes Christians generous with their person, purse, and property (verse 13). We do not begrudge the extra time and effort which entertaining friends involves. We welcome guests not just because we can't get out of it graciously but because showing hospitality to God's people is service rendered to Christ. The spirit works such a transformation in the attitudes of Christians that we are considerate even of those who persecute us for Jesus' sake (verse 14). They attack our character and malign our motives, and we say, "May God bless you, neighbor." That kind of response is the result of the Spirit's operation in the soul.

As we make progress in sanctification, our sympathetic nature is affected. We really do feel like rejoicing when another Christian receives spiritual blessings or temporal benefits while we go without (verse 15). When distresses and calamities overtake fellow believers, we feel their sorrow in the depths of our being. We experience this concord not only in what we mutually feel but also in what we mutually think (verse 16). We certainly do not

quality; they are the product of the Spirit's influences upon the soul.

Philippians 2:1-8 is a commentary on

likemindedness.
See also
Philippians 4:2.

see eye-to-eye on every issue, but generally speaking, our outlook is the same because the same Spirit is transforming our minds so that more and more they harmonize with the mind of Christ. A sanctified mind is neither snobbish nor sophisticated. We do not look down on common people. A sanctified mind is not opinionated. We do not imagine that we know more than anyone else and that our advice is the only advice worth listening to.

ETHICAL RELATIONSHIPS
OUTSIDE THE FAMILY
(Romans 12:17—13:7)

It is a mistake to think that we are perfectly obedient, perfectly submissive, or perfectly yielded. We aim for this, but we shall not attain it. Even Paul never arrived at perfection (Philippians 3:12).

Remember, Christians are in the process of being transformed. We obey none of the commands of Romans 12 perfectly, although it is our duty to do so. It is our duty to cooperate with all of the inward workings of the Holy Spirit. All of the results however, redound to the Spirit's credit, and what marvelous results they are! They affect all of our relationships with God, with ourselves, with our Christian brothers and sisters, and now, we learn, with our enemies. Sanctification gradually takes away our natural inclination to pay back meanness with meanness (verse 17). It prompts us to live aboveboard so that the unsaved will not have any reason to find fault with our behavior.

"Live in peace; and the God of love and peace shall be with you" (II Corinthians 13:11).

The gentle dove of peace, the Holy Spirit, resides in us to make us peacemakers, not troublemakers (verse 18). Love of tranquility and abhorrence for loud and noisy rackets are evidences of sanctification. We strive never to disturb the peace. One of the surest methods to get a fight started is to take divine vengeance into our own hands, and so we take a hands-off policy (verse 19). Let God repay our enemeies as and when He wills. We take special pains to make a friend out of the enemy by repaying hostility with loving deeds (verse 20). Hopefully the enemy will become ashamed of himself and repent of his animosity. When this occurs, we have triumphed over his evil by our good (verse 21).

Progressive sanctification makes us obedient to civil authority—and to all authority (13:1). God commands it, and the Spirit enables us to comply by putting a disposition of submissiveness in us. Rather than breaking the laws of the land, we uphold them. When we feel that our government is doing a poor job, we act in a lawful manner to correct the situation. We voice our concerns at the election polls and in correspondence with our elected officials. At all times we act in a peaceful way. Whoever resorts to criminal or subversive activity deserves to be punished (verse 2).

Government is responsible to serve municipal, county, state, and national interests. It works for our safety—to protect citizens against criminal elements and foreign aggression (verse 3). If we behave ourselves, we have no reason to fear the cop on the corner. Law-abiding people enjoy a good standing in the community. They know that laws are necessary for their welfare, and they appreciate law-enforcement agencies which have the right to deal with lawbreakers, even to the extent of inflicting the death penalty upon them (verse 4).

Christians obey the laws of the land because it is God's will and because it is right (verse 5). It is a sad day when we comply with traffic regulations just because we fear the consequences of getting caught. When Christians cooperate with the

Consider Jesus' instructions in Matthew 5:38-44.

Our space age is typically an age of lawlessness. Lawlessness is the spirit of antichrist. For a Christian to participate in any lawless activity is for him to take sides with antichrist.

On the Christian's duty toward government, see I Timothy 2:1-3; I Peter 2:13-17.

leading of the Spirit in His sanctifying work, they pay their taxes and show a reverential respect to everyone who holds a public office (verses 6,7).

NOW TEST YOUR KNOWLEDGE

Give short answers:

1. What three parts of man does sanctification affect? _____

2. What contributes nothing to sanctification? _____

3. What power changes our minds, feelings, and will? _____

4. What gifts are in vogue among Christians today? _____

5. What kind of zeal is the only safe zeal? _____

6. What is the will of God for us? _____

7. How does sanctification affect the mind? _____

8. How does sanctification affect the emotions? _____

9. How does sanctification affect the will? _____

10. What responsibility do we owe government? _____

How far should we go in our effort to maintain peace? Why can't we work for peace at any price? What have we no right to sacrifice in the cause of peace?

FOOD FOR THOUGHT

"Evangelical faith without Christian ethics is a travesty on the gospel."
—V. Raymond Edman

YOU CANNOT HAVE YOUR OWN WAY

11

LESSON SCRIPTURE
Romans 13:8—15:6.

RELATED SCRIPTURE
I Corinthians 8:1-13; 10:23-33;
Galatians 5:1-16.

LESSON AIM
To uphold the principle of love as the only sufficient motive for right conduct; to draft Biblical guidelines for deciding questions of personal scruples.

LEARN BY HEART
"Whether therefore ye eat, or drink, or whatsoever ye do, do all to the glory of God" (I Corinthians 10:31).

EVERY DAY WITH THE WORD

Monday	Weak knees	Psalm 109:22-31
Tuesday	Weak hands	Isaiah 35:3-10
Wednesday	Weak flesh	Romans 8:1-9
Thursday	Weak things	I Corinthians 1:26-31
Friday	Weak conscience	I Corinthians 8:1-13
Saturday	Weak presence	II Corinthians 10:7-18
Sunday	Weak elements	Galatians 4:8-18

STUDENT'S NOTEBOOK

This column is for the student who desires additional study of the lesson theme.

LESSON PREPARATION

"Love shall cover the multitude of sins" (I Peter 4:8)—an interesting text, but what does it mean? It suggests that the love which God has put in the Christian's heart enables him to overlook the faults, frailties, and foibles of other Christians. For love's sake, we refuse to make an issue

Let me be a little kinder;
Let me be a little blinder
To the faults of those about me;
Let me praise a little more.

over the defects which we see in others. That same love makes us long-suffering and forbearing toward each other (Ephesians 4:2). It prompts us to do everything possible to maintain "the unity of the Spirit in the bond of peace."

THE DISPOSITION OF LOVE
(Romans 13:8-14)

Love is the most effective legislator for every aspect of the believer's life. It spares us from chronic indebtedness—from getting so deep into financial obligations that we have no prospect of ever getting out (verse 8). Love pays its debt to creditors. The Christian who has any regard at all for his family or his friends will keep his financial affairs in good order.

If we would always act toward each other in love, there would be no need for laws; we would automatically fulfill the law's requirements and then some. You wouldn't need legislation forbidding adultery, murder, theft, slander, covetousness, and a thousand other crimes if we all loved each other as we love ourselves (verse 9). The law prohibits these things, but only genuine love in the heart takes away a man's desire to commit such sins against his neighbor (verse 10).

To love our neighbor as ourselves means to be as solicitous about his welfare as we are about our own, to be as eager to see him succeed as we are eager to succeed, to protect his reputation as earnestly as we protect our own, and to be as concerned about the salvation of his soul as we are about our own salvation. That kind of love is supernatural, but it is the only kind of which God approves and which assures us of social tranquility.

Even the mosaic law presupposes that love is the motivating principle behind conformity to its rigid demands

(Deuteronomy 6:5; 10:18,19). See Matthew 19:19,22.

The law of love toward neighbors is pictured in the parable of the Good Samaritan (Luke 10:30-37).

In the account of the Good Samaritan the object of love was a member of another race against whom Jews discriminated.

89

This kind of love is all the more necessary in view of the lateness of the hour in which we now live. For us the day of final deliverance is near, but has our indifference and lack of love ill-prepared the neighbors for the coming of Christ? We have only a short time left in which to witness of His saving grace. We need to rub sleep from our eyes and become more alert to our opportunities (verse 11). We want to be sure that no wicked deeds in us are a cause of a neighbor's not coming to Christ. He is quick to see imperfections in us, to say nothing of immorality if it lurks there. Let's jump out of our night shirt and dress up for daylight fighting (verse 12). Let's defy the neighbors to find any trace of impiety, impurity, or insobriety in us (verse 13). Let's be done with petty quarreling and jealousies.

"Awake thou that sleepest, and arise from the dead, and Christ shall give thee light" (Ephesians 5:14).

We need to become so absorbed with Christ's interests, enter so thoroughly into His views, and respond so exemplarily to our critical times—in short, to be Christ's follower from head to toe—that those who observe us will be continually reminded of Him (verse 14). He wants us to put on all of the virtues that characterized Him. Nothing works so effectively to keep us from scheming how we can gratify our sinful lusts.

We are clothed from head to foot in Christ's righteousness, and so we should act righteously from head to heel.

THE DECISIONS OF LOVE
(Romans 14:1—15:6)

It comes as a surprise to some Christians that the New Testament does not lay down a clear-cut rule to govern every moral decision. The Pharisees had such a codebook, but the Bible does not regulate every hour of the day for Christians. Some believers, it appears, would be happier if it

Knowing the will
of God in
matters of
current trends is
not as easy as
some would lead
you to believe.
We must always
be testing
debatable issues.

did, for then they would be obliged to do no thinking or praying, and they could have the satisfaction of attaining spirituality by rigid adherence to
religious law.

The silence of the New Testament about hundreds of moral decisions facing today's Christian
has given rise to great differences of opinion
among Bible-believers. Here are some of the issues
on which the New Testament makes no comment:
Sunday activities (buying and selling, sports,
amusements), dress and styles (shorts, slacks, for
women, long hair for men), eating or trading
where liquor is sold, cultural events (modern art,
drama, literature, music), entertainment (roller
skating, bowling, square dancing or folk dancing,
mixed bathing, card playing, movies, TV), and
foods (especially wine and other alcoholic
beverages). The list is almost endless. Various sec-
tions of the country and the world have special
preferences. How are we going to come to a
meeting of the minds on these differences, or shall
we just fight it out to the bitter end?

The love that
distinguishes
Christians is
stronger than the
differences
which divide
them.

I Corinthians
8:1-13; 10:23-33
all deal with
general
principles which
apply to our
liberty in Christ.

The Bible gives general principles and guidelines
to help each Christian decide these issues for
himself. The first principle says, act with your
liberty in Christ in view. Many of our differences
are owing to personal taste. God has not made us
all alike. If the Bible does not forbid it, you are
free to do it (Romans 14:2). All things are lawful
for me (I Corinthians 6:12). God has created all
things for us to enjoy. The mature Christian ap-
preciates this truth and acts upon it. The immature
Christian thinks he is obligated to adhere to
various religious taboos which characterize his
fellowship of churches and he acts accordingly.

When people
hold to
abstinence as an

Two groups of Christians can be found in most

churches: those who indulge and those who abstain. Each has an obligation to the other. The indulgers have no right to belittle the narrowmindedness of the abstainers, and the abstainers have no right to pass snap judgments upon the broadmindedness of the indulgers (verse 3). In all of the questionable activities that present themselves to us, each of us must be convinced in his own mind whether it is right or wrong (verse 5). One of the great truths of the New Testament is soul liberty. Our conduct is not monitored by our church but by the Holy Spirit. We do what we think is right for us, not what others think is right for us. If we participate in an activity or observe some occasion with a spirit of thankfulness to God and with a view to glorifying Him, we are perfectly free to do so (verse 6)—even though some other Christians frown on these things and find it impossible to glorify God by engaging in them.

One of the crucial factors in deciding these doubtful issues is the lordship of Christ. Whatever we do reflects upon Him for good or ill. He owns us by redemptive purchase, and we owe Him our obedience (verses 7-9). You have to consider whether the practice you are engaging in is gaining mastery over you. If it is, you will have to give it up because it is undermining Christ's right alone to master you. If you find that you cannot live without your coffee or some other stimulant or depressant, and you cannot live without your golf or some other amusement, then you are in servitude to something other than to Christ and in the process have really lost your liberty in Christ. Act, therefore, with the lordship of Christ in view.

Act with the judgment seat of Christ in view (verse 10). On this awesome occasion Christ will

essential for salvation, then their defect enters the category of heresy. This was the danger which the Colossian church faced with the Gnostics (Colossians 2:20-23).

"Nothing is to be refused, if it is received with thanksgiving; for it is sanctified by the word of God and prayer" (I Timothy 4:4,5). This rule does not apply to what the Word of God expressly forbids.

We must say with Paul, "I will not be brought under the power of any" (I Corinthians 6:12,13).

II Corinthians 5:10

review our attitudes toward other Christians and award us accordingly. If we have been accustomed to making others feel small by our superior airs and our uninhibited exercise of Christian liberty, we shall have to answer to Christ for it. In that day everyone will have to acknowledge Christ's unerring justice in making all things right (verse 11). When we realize we shall have to give an account for every idle word and deed, we think twice before we speak and perform (verse 12).

Act with the weaknesses of others in view (verse 13). God judges our actions by the effect they have upon someone else. We cannot do everything that our liberties in Christ permit because the uninstructed Christian who has convictions about these things will be shocked by our actions. We must forfeit our rights rather than dull another Christian's moral sensitivity or draw him into what he thinks is sin. Love smooths the way; it does not stack stones in another Christian's path over which he may stumble to his spiritual injury.

Hundreds of practices are neither immoral nor moral; they are amoral—outside the sphere to which moral judgments apply. But if some conscientious Christian thinks a certain practice is immoral, then for him it is immoral until the Holy Spirit enlightens his conscience to see that it is not immoral (verse 14). Meanwhile, he must act according to what light his conscience has, and we who know better must not goad him into acting contrary to his conscience. Furthermore, we have to exercise the greatest care not to practice the very things that we know will offend the weak conscience of another believer. It will not do us any harm to give them up, but it may do others great harm if we don't (verse 15).

Matthew 12:36

Jesus had some very severe things to say about people who offended God's little children (Matthew 18:6-10).

In regeneration the conscience is purified, but it does not thereby become a perfect judge of all conduct. If the conscience were an infallible guide, we would not need to Word of God or the Spirit of God.

The main aim of the Christian life is to promote righteousness, peace, and joy (verse 17). Whatever practices do not contribute to this end have little or no value. They add nothing to acceptable service for Christ (verse 18). We must act with Christ's approval in view. Peace does enhance our service, and so it is better to forfeit our liberties if by doing so we can maintain tranquility in the church (verse 19). We must learn to follow a course of action that will not unnecessarily stir up a controversy over nonessentials. Act in such a way that your behavior edifies the church. Standing up for your rights is hardly an edifying ministry when it results in the downfall of other Christians (verses 20,21).

We cannot, however, maintain peace at any price. We cannot make peace with the devil or with heretical ministers, or with erring saints. On matters of personal scruples, we can agree to disagree and still have good fellowship one with another.

Act in faith (verses 22,23). If you have uneasy feelings about a certain practice, then you must not engage in it. Whatever we do that is not motivated by faith is sinful. If you have no qualms about it, then enjoy it—if, of course, other considerations make it advisable.

Act with the example of Christ in view (Romans 15:1-3). Look at what He put up with in dealing with our infirmities. Think of the limitations He imposed upon Himself in order to redeem us. He never gave a thought to doing what He pleased. He always pleased the Father—"Not my will but thine be done." If we truly follow Him, this will be our attitude in forfeiting our rights rather than in pleasing ourselves and with it run roughshod over a weaker Christian.

Act with the Scripture in view (verses 4-6). The Old Testament Scriptures cite the patience of Job and other saints in order to encourage us to exercise patience. It is going to require a lot of patience to fellowship with Christians whose immaturity gets under our skin. We need patience in order not to run selfishly on our way in the strength of our more enlightened convictions while they faint along the way for not having the courage to keep up with us. And we are going to need a lot of supernatural know-how in order to comfort and console the weaker brethren who despair of ever attaining the character of the strong.

Where is this kind of patience and consolation going to come from? We must count on the God of patience and the God of all comfort to give us the kind of attitudes that are necessary for resolving the many differences that distinguish us, so that with one mind and mouth we can all glorify our God and His Son, our Saviour. In this like-mindedness we are still growing.

FOOD FOR THOUGHT

"In essentials, unity; in nonessentials, liberty; in all things, charity."

—Selected

NOW TEST YOUR KNOWLEDGE

Fill in the blanks:

1. There would be no need for laws if we always acted in _____.

2. For God to approve of our affections, our love must be_____.

3. Nothing works so effectively to keep us from gratifying our lusts as _____.

4. The Bible does not lay down specific rules for regulating all our conduct, but it does give _____.

5. Deciding the issues calls for the great New Testament truth, _____.

6. A crucial factor in deciding doubtful matters is _____.

7. We must all stand before_____to give an account.

8. If a practice is neither moral nor immoral, it is _____.

9. We must always act according to the light of _____.

10. The main aim of the Christian life is to promote _____, _____, and _____.

11. All acts are sinful if they are not motivated by _____.

12. In order to fellowship with immature Christians we have special need of _____.

YOU ARE A CO-LABORER WITH CHRIST

12

LESSON SCRIPTURE
Romans 15:7-33

RELATED SCRIPTURE
Isaiah 66:10-20; II Timothy 4:17,18;
Hebrews 3:1-6; 8:1-5.

LESSON AIM
To find in Christ our example for an
acceptable ministry; to determine
what place the Holy Spirit, personal
desire, prayer, and Christian
fellowship have in the ministry.

LEARN BY HEART
"Now the God of hope fill you with
all joy and peace in believing, that
ye may abound in hope, through the
power of the Holy Ghost" (Romans
15:13).

EVERY DAY WITH THE WORD

Monday	Assistant minister	Acts 13:1-5
Tuesday	Attentive ministers	Romans 13:1-6
Wednesday	Accountable ministers	I Corinthians 4:1-5
Thursday	Able ministers	II Corinthians 3:6-18
Friday	Approved ministers	II Corinthians 6:1-10
Saturday	Appointed minister	Ephesians 3:1-12
Sunday	Angelic ministers	Hebrews 1:1-14

LESSON PREPARATION

It is a high
calling
(Philippians 3:14).

A wise man noted that the ministry of the gospel
is the poorest of trades but the noblest of callings.
Chapter 15 of Romans brings together some con-
cluding facts that will help us to pursue our calling
with the same diligence which the Lord Jesus
Christ pursued His. He remains forever as the

Ephesians 5:1,2

model servant of Jehovah. We must study Him
and copy His devotion to service.

THE MINISTRY OF JESUS CHRIST
(Romans 15:7-13)

In his instructions to the church at Rome Paul
has been telling them to receive immature Christians without restraint. We have no right to bar
them from fellowship just because their moral
scruples differ from ours. Even weak believers
have a right to expect our confidence and feel our
love. When we were without strength, Christ loved
us, gave Himself for us, and was unashamed to
own us as His property and His responsibility. He
received us with a view to conforming us to God's
glory (verse 7). Likewise, we cordially embrace the
weaker brethren and work toward bringing them
to glorify God.

We fellowship in
doctrine (Acts
2:42), in the Son
(I Corinthians
1:9), in the
gospel
(Philippians 1:5),
in the Spirit
(Philippians 2:1),
in suffering
(Philippians 3:10.)
Our fellowship is
with the Father
and His Son
(I John 1:3).

Jesus Christ was a minister—one who served
voluntarily in order to vindicate the truth of God's
promises to the patriarchs (verse 8). He came to
the Jewish nation and became obedient unto death
in order to convey to them the blessings of
justification which God promised to Abraham's
heirs. Preeminently, Jesus directed His ministry to
the lost sheep of the house of Israel. But this ex-
clusive service was not an end in itself; He had a
much wider ministry in view among the Gentiles
(verse 9). In other words, Christ's special work
with respect to Israel was a means toward another
end—namely, the salvation of the Gentiles.

Mark 10:45

Galatians 3:14

Matthew 10:6

"Other sheep I
have, that are
not of this
[Jewish] fold"
(John 10:16).

All during the time that God was dealing almost
exclusively with Jews, He nevertheless instructed
Israel in His ultimate intent for Gentiles. God did
not forget the nations whom He had abandoned to
their pagan vices. He planned through Israel's

The Old Testament frequently speaks of the salvation of the Gentiles. It never suggests, however, that saved Gentiles would be equal to Jews. Gentile equality belongs to the New Testament revelation. See Ephesians 3:5,6.

Messiah to have mercy on the Gentiles. Gentiles were destined to participate in Israel's joy and praise (verses 9,10). Isaiah predicted that Gentiles as a whole would one day acknowledge the heir to David's throne and trust him for their salvation and safety (verse 12). The Abrahamic promise included Gentiles, but the promises have had only a partial fulfillment during the church age. In the coming millennial kingdom the great mass of Gentiles will at last become the recipients of Abrahamic spiritual blessings and also share in Israel's material prosperity.

The ministry of Christ gives Gentiles as well as Jews reason to hope. We are begotten to a living hope by the resurrection of Jesus Christ from the dead (I Peter 1:3). God the Father is the author and source of our hope; He causes us to abound in this virtue (verse 13). The power of the Holy Spirit activates and generates hope in us. The effect of hope is a joyous peace. This kind of hope enables us to feel joy in the company of even the weaker brethren, and it maintains a settled calm in the camp even though Christians continue to have their differences.

THE MINISTER OF JESUS CHRIST
(Romans 15:14-33)

The minister of the circumcision—Jesus Christ—had appointed Paul to be a minister to the uncircumcision. Paul's epistle to the church at Rome was part of his mission to the Gentiles. He wrote directions to them not because he had founded the church (he hadn't), not because they were incapable of admonishing each other, but because the gracious influences of the Holy Spirit

Peter, James, and John were appointed to minister to the circumcision— that is, to the Jews (Galatians 2:7-9).

had prompted him to stir up their minds by way of remembrance. They were well qualified to minister to each other because they possessed the virtues of goodness and knowledge (verse 14). Knowledge enabled them to instruct the weak; goodness prevented them from taking advantage of the weak.

Remember, in Romans the weak are those who have not come into the enjoyment of their liberties in Christ.

If Paul appears to speak too unreservedly and authoritatively to a group of Christians whom he had never met and whose church he had no part in founding, the grace of God is responsible for it (verse 15). After all, he had the special distinction of being the apostle to the Gentiles, and Rome was within the territory which God had assigned to him. He had no ambition to order the Romans around; he intended only to offer them up to God as an acceptable sacrifice (verse 16). To be acceptable, they had to be holy, and what Paul taught them was geared to make them holy. Gentiles sanctified by the Holy Spirit were truly holy as opposed to Jews who practiced circumcision but experienced no sanctifying influences of the Spirit. Gentiles were a sanctified offering even though they were uncircumcised and in the Jewish view, therefore, unclean.

In verse 16, notice the Trinity in unity.

Acts 15:9 says that God purified the hearts of the Gentiles by faith.

Paul took special delight in Gentile salvation, Gentile holiness, Gentile liberties, and Gentile obedience. He boasted of what the gospel had done for Gentiles despite the opposition of legalistic Jews (verse 17). All of Paul's accomplishments in Gentile territory gave him no occasion to brag about himself (verse 18). In himself he was as weak as any other mortal. When the Gentiles obeyed the gospel as the result of hearing Paul's words and witnessing his deeds, it was Christ who got the glory, not Paul.

It was the power of the Holy Spirit which brought the Gentiles to obedience (verses 18,19). Paul had no power in himself to command such submission to Christ.

When Paul cast out a demon, healed the sick, raised the dead, and worked other special miracles, he did so by the power of the Holy Spirit, not by his own power (verse 19). From Jerusalem to Illyricum his ministry was attended by the most convincing proofs of his apostleship and authority. The same Spirit who enabled him to perform signs and wonders also enabled him to preach the gospel fully. Preaching messages requires no less power than performing miracles. All of the densely populated centers along the principal Roman routes had heard the gospel which Paul preached.

Preaching and praying are both strenuous activities. Compare verses 20 and 30. Note the word "strive."

In the discharge of his commission to Gentiles, Paul avoided those areas where a church had already sprung up as the result of the evangelistic endeavors of other men (verse 20). He felt no impetus of the Spirit to start a competitive work. Furthermore, he had no leading of the Spirit to become the pastor of a church which another man had founded. God called him to do pioneer missionary work, and this was the unalterable direction of his whole life. He knew he had been called to enlighten the minds of Gentiles and bring them face to face with Christ (verse 21).

Until that work was done, Paul could not rest, and he could not pay a long-awaited visit to the saints in Rome (verse 22). Evangelizing the eastern half of the Roman Empire kept him so busy that he had not been able to work a Roman tour into his schedule. Evidently his circumstances were changing. He came to see that his work was finished in the Near East (verse 23). It was becoming more and more dangerous for him to remain in areas where unbelieving Jews dogged his footsteps and stirred up hostility against him. The time was

As much as he longed to see the Roman Christians, Paul always put first things first.

now favorable for him to fulfill his desire to see the Roman Christians.

The journey to Rome, however, was only a means to an end. Paul's real objective was the Roman province of Spain. A vast territory lay in the extreme West which had never felt the impact of the gospel. En route to Spain (perhaps Britain was also in his sights) Paul would pause at Rome long enough to enlist their support of the project and then proceed with his plan to take Christ to another place where He was unknown and unacknowledged (verse 24). Fellowshiping with the church at Rome would provide both psychological and spiritual preparation for the excursion to Spain.

At the moment, however, Paul felt that he must postpone the visit just a little longer—long enough for him to make a hurried trip to Jerusalem (verse 25). The Greek churches had been collecting relief money for the destitute Jewish Christians in the holy city, and Paul was eager to carry the funds to Jerusalem. He had never forgotten the promise which he made at the council in Jerusalem in A.D. 50. He had assured the Jewish party that he would remember the poor. In the Galatian epistle Paul adds, "The same which I also was forward to do" (2:10). He wasn't one to back down on a promise.

Verse 26 is the key to the date when Paul wrote the epistle to the Romans. He was in Macedonia and Achaia for the purpose of receiving the offerings which the churches had been collecting for the Jews. This coincides with Acts 20:1-5. He wrote Romans sometime during the three-month residence at Corinth—the winter of A.D. 56-57—just as he was completing a third missionary journey. The Macedonian churches were not wealthy, but

By telling the Romans he was taking a contribution to the saints in Jerusalem, Paul was indirectly giving the Romans inspiration to support his new expedition to Spain.

they gave liberally and lovingly because they sensed how much they owed spiritually to the church at Jerusalem (verse 27). The money, Paul hoped, would convince the Jewish church of the love which the Greek churches felt toward them (verse 28). Material assistance would tighten the bond of fellowship between them.

The mission complete, Paul intended to come directly to Rome in the full blessing of grace and power (verse 29). He would discharge this final duty toward the East before embarking upon a new enterprise in the West. In the intervening months before he would arrive in Rome, he needed especially the prayers of the Roman Christians (verse 30). He asks them to wrestle in prayer on his behalf. He appeals to them to do it for Jesus' sake and because of the Spirit's love. He requests prayer for his deliverance from the Jewish opposition; he anticipates that godless Jews will make an attempt on his life. He solicits prayer that the Christian Jews will receive the relief money (verse 31). He knew that religious prejudice against Gentiles might cause Jews to refuse the gift. They might cut off their noses to spite their faces.

Finally, Paul covets their prayers that his hope of reaching Rome will materialize, that he will arrive as God willed, and that joy and refreshment will be his experience (verse 32). All of these prayers were answered—not in the way Paul expected but nevertheless answered. He was delivered from the Jewish mob who tried to kill him in Jerusalem. He did arrive safely in Rome although he was under military escort at the time and although he had had to pass two dreary years in prison at Caesarea. All of these eventualities were part of the plan of God.

Paul prayed for the Roman Christians (verse 33). He requested that the God of peace would heal all divisions between the weak and the strong.

NOW TEST YOUR KNOWLEDGE

How does believing prayer change things? Or, does it just change people? What is the relationship of prayer to God's work and will?

Find the answers in Romans 15:

1. How many times do you find references to "minister" or "ministering"? _____

2. What three prominent titles of God do you find? _____

3. How many references do you find to the Holy Spirit? _____

4. What two virtues do we need in order to admonish other Christians? _____

5. What were the geographical limits of Paul's preaching in the East? _____

6. How many references to Jerusalem do you find? _____

7. Where did Paul want to begin a new ministry? _____

8. What did Paul take to the saints at Jerusalem? _____

9. Which verses speak of joy and peace? _____ _____

10. What enabled Paul to write boldly to the Romans? _____

FOOD FOR THOUGHT

"You do not do God a favor by serving Him. He honors you by allowing you to serve Him."

—Victor Nyquist

GOD KNOWS YOU BY NAME

13

LESSON SCRIPTURE
Romans 16:1-27

RELATED SCRIPTURE
Ephesians 2:11—3:12;
Colossians 1:24-27;
II John 1,5,13.

LESSON AIM
To evaluate our friendships and
remember the labors of others on
our behalf; to discern how the grace
of God ensures unity and harmony
in the churches.

LEARN BY HEART
"And the God of peace shall bruise
Satan under your feet shortly. The
grace of our Lord Jesus Christ be
with you. Amen" (Romans 16:20).

STUDENT'S NOTEBOOK

This column is for
the student who
desires additional
study of the lesson
theme.

EVERY DAY WITH THE WORD

Monday	A pitiless friend	Job 19:1-29
Tuesday	A familiar friend	Psalm 41:1-13
Wednesday	A loving friend	Proverbs 17:17-28
Thursday	A faithful friend	Proverbs 27:1-10
Friday	A beloved friend	Song of Solomon 5:10-16
Saturday	An importunate friend	Luke 11:5-10
Sunday	An obedient friend	John 15:9-17

LESSON PREPARATION

Count how many
times Paul uses
the word
"beloved" in
Romans 16.

At first glance you might think the epistle to the
Romans is only a theological treatise and that
Christianity is a dogmatic religion which for the
most part attracts scholars. Chapter 16 certainly
puts Christianity in an entirely different light. It is

intensely personal, as a long list of enduring acquaintances and endearing terms shows.

PERSONAL GREETINGS
(Romans 16:1-16)

It is significant that a woman stands at the top of Paul's list of helpers, friends, relatives, and early converts. For one thing, it proves that Paul was no woman-hater, as his critics have charged. The fact that Phebe was a "servant" in the church indicates that women are not excluded from Christian work in the church (verse 1). In all likelihood, Phebe was a wealthy widow who gave her time and money to the cause of the sick, the poor, the orphaned, the disconsolate, and the stranger. Many believe that Paul entrusted her to deliver the epistle to the Romans. In that case, she was a highly responsible woman who had earned a place of trust.

From verse 2 we presume Phebe was a business woman and that the transaction of private affairs required her presence in Rome. W. J. Conybeare thinks she was involved in a lawsuit. Paul urged the Roman Christians to assist her in every way possible. We may infer that Christianity is not incompatible with the pursuit of business interests; in fact, Christianity directs business toward a spiritual end. Phebe is the first person whom Paul acknowledges with grateful appreciation for her ministry on his behalf.

Priscilla and Aquila are among the famous personalities of the New Testament (verse 3). "Priscilla" is the informal form of "Prisca," meaning "ancient." She probably descended from an old Roman family and had, therefore, some distinguished status. Her husband Aquila, mean-

Although the word "servant" here can be rendered "deaconess," it is doubtful that Phebe held the office of a deaconess. It is doubtful that such an office existed in the early church.

You might want to reflect upon the problem of when business becomes a hindrance to the Christian life.

ing "eagle," was a Jew from Pontus. They were professionals in leathercraft and probably occupied a large home in Corinth and Ephesus, where they made their accommodations available for a Christian assembly. When Paul first visited Corinth, he resided with Priscilla and Aquila and plied his trade in partnership with them.

Perhaps it was at Corinth or Ephesus where this godly couple endangered their own lives in order to secure Paul's safety (verse 4). Not only Paul but all of the Gentile churches who knew the circumstances felt a deep sense of gratitude to Priscilla and Aquila for the risk they ran. Whatever we do for any servant of God we do for the whole church of Christ.

Epaenetus was the first soul whom Paul led to Christ in Asia (verse 5). The reading "Achaia" is probably not accurate. The household of Stephanas were the first converts of Paul in Achaia. If the reading "Achaia" is correct, then Epaenetus must have been a member of Stephanas' household. "Epaenetus" means "laudable." Mary had worn herself out in long service to others (verse 6). A few manuscripts have "you" instead of "us." This would mean that Paul was commending her for her labors in the church at Rome. Paul was evidently well-posted on the activities of the saints around the Roman world.

Andronicus and Junia were relatives of Paul who had seniority in grace (verse 7). They were believers at the time when Paul was still persecuting the church. Perhaps their prayers for Paul were instrumental in his conversion. At some time or another they were prisoners with Paul. Their steadfast adherence to the faith despite opposition gave them a place of distinction. The apostles themselves took note of the gifts and graces of this illustrious husband and wife.

Ampliatus, whose name means "enlarged," is otherwise wholly unknown to us (verse 8). He was dear to Paul. Urbanus is equally elusive (verse 9). His name signifies "pleasant" or "city-bred." At some point he had worked together with Paul. "Stachys" is a Greek name, meaning "ear of grain." The man who bore it was loved by Paul, but other than this we know nothing about him. "Apelles" occurs frequently in Imperial household circles and suggests that this approved servant of Christ may have won the esteem of his Christian brethren by overcoming some temptation in the Imperial palace (verse 10). We do not know that Aristobulus himself was a Christian, but many if not all of the slaves in his service belonged to Christ. "Aristobulus" means "best counselor."

Herodion was probably related to the family of the Herods (verse 11). He might have been a member of Aristobulus' household. He was either a relative of Paul or at least a fellow Jew. Narcissus was another slaveholder whose staff numbered several Christians. "Narcissus" means "benumbing." Tryphena and Typhosa were relatives or sisters, possibly twin sisters (verse 12). Both names suggest what is delicate or accustomed to luxury. These ladies labored to the point of exhaustion for the Lord. Persis gave the same tireless and toilsome service to Christ while her strength remained. Her name indicates that she may have come from Persia.

"Rufus" means "red." The bearer of the name may have had red hair. He was certainly a choice Christian who had rendered excellent service

If Andronicus and Junia were apostles, as some say, then they were lesser apostles like Barnabas and not the chief apostles like the twelve.

In verse 10, the word "approved" indicates that Apelles had endured some rigorous test and shown himself equal to it. He emerged as fine gold, his faith purified in the fire.

Note that Paul does not call a lady "my" beloved. He refers to her as "the" beloved. Do you think Paul used good taste?

(verse 13). Mark 15:21 gives us reason to think he was one of the sons of Simon of Cyrene. How Simon, a dark-skinned father, could have a red-haired son is a problem for the geneticist to figure out. It is not impossible. Rufus' mother took Paul under her maternal wing at a time perhaps when both Paul's father and mother had disowned him for turning to Christ.

"Asyncritus," "incomparable"; "Phlegon," "zealous burning"; "Hermes," the name of the god of luck; "Patrobas," (?); and "Hermas," a variation of "Hermes"—all are names associated with one of the churches in Rome, of which there were possibly five at the time. Philologus and his wife Julia lent their home to one of these Christian assemblies (verse 15). "Philologus" means "talkative," and we can imagine that after his conversion he did a lot of talking about Christ. Nereus was named after the Greek sea-god. He and his sister were members of the church which met in Philologus' home. "Olympas" may mean "bright." The man who bore the name had an opportunity to shine for Jesus.

The personalities whom Paul and the Gentile churches greeted represent every strata of Roman society. They include men and women, slaves and freemen, old and young, rich and poor, married and widowed, brothers and sisters by blood and by grace, the well-known and the unknown, the distinguished and the obscure. All of these Christians exchanged the holy kiss as a token of their fellowship in Christ (verse 16).

PLENTIFUL GRACE
(Romans 16:17-27)

Nothing short of the supernatural operation of grace in the soul is sufficient to keep the bond of

---

Paul declared that he had suffered the loss of all things for Christ. He most likely lost his parents and his inheritance. Some interpreters go so far as to say he lost his wife.

peace in an assembly that incorporated such a wide variety of personalities and backgrounds. When masters greet slaves with the kiss of peace, you know God's grace alone is responsible for it. The maintenance of unity and harmony is the gracious work of the Spirit, but this excuses no one from working at it diligently. Paul knew human nature well enough to anticipate that a certain group of fleshly church members would cause rifts and ruptures whenever and wherever they could. He advised the church at Rome to label those who sow discord and stray from doctrine (verse 17). By God's grace we must stay away from such people lest we be influenced by their subtleties and injured in the snares they set for us.

Men who drive wedges between the saints think only of themselves—how to satisfy their personal whims and indulge their base instincts (verse 18). They are adept at expressing themselves in such a way as to deceive the unwary. They appear suave and smooth, but their real motives are selfish and sensual. A Roman Christian might be an easy victim to tall talkers because of his natural inclination towards obedience (verse 19). We need divine wisdom and grace to know what we should obey and what we should refuse to obey. We do not want to be overly suspicious, and yet we cannot heed every voice that calls.

Satan is the power behind all schisms and spats in the church. He is determined to break the peace. We need grace to look to the God of peace to preserve the unity of the body of Christ (verse 20).

Timothy, Lucius, Jason, and Sosipater were all with Paul when he penned Romans (verse 21). They were in his company on the eve of his depar-

> Note the variety of racial backgrounds in the Roman church: Greeks, Italians, Persians, blacks (Rufus), Jews. Grace can enable different people to fellowship together in peace.

> Compare Romans 16:18 with Philippians 3:18,19.

> Ephesians 4:3 recognizes that it takes an effort on the part of Christians to preserve church unity.

ture to Jerusalem with the collection. Aristarchus and Secundus of Thessalonica, Gaius of Derbe, and Tychicus and Trophimus of Ephesus were also in the party (Acts 20:4). Many of these men accompanied him to Jerusalem, acting in the capacity of companions, delegates, and body-guards. Tertius, whole name means "third," served as Paul's private secretary in the writing of the epistle to the Romans (verses 22).

Another Gaius was also hospitable (III John 1,5,6).

Paul was a guest in the home of Gaius of Corinth at the time—a home which was always open to visiting Christians (verse 23). Erastus held a prominent public office at Corinth. Quartus whose name means "fourth," may have been a brother of Tertius. All of these men were brothers in Christ as the result of the grace of Christ, who is our

Hebrews 2:11

brother (verse 24).

The same grace that unites the people of God also undergirds them. The power of grace stablishes, stabilizes, supports, and strengthens the believer (verse 25). The gospel of grace is God's instrument for bringing to effect not only our salvation but our growth in sanctification. This gospel had its mighty effect especially upon Gentiles to whom Paul presented the claims of Christ. In all of Paul's preaching he kept clearly in view what had been undisclosed to former generations—namely, that Gentiles had equal status with the Jews in the church of God.

When Gentiles obey the gospel of Christ, they receive full and equal citizenship. In the church there are no second-class citizens. If we are to understand Gentile equality in the body, we must draw our wisdom from the only wise God whose all-wise plan included the Gentiles and whose only Son is the perfect mediator for once-estranged

Gentiles (verse 27). From that God we receive grace to submit to His purposes and to Him we ascribe all glory, laud, and honor.

NOW TEST YOUR KNOWLEDGE

Match names with identifications:

__ 1. Born and bred in the city

__ 2. Twin sisters

__ 3. Relatives of Paul

__ 4. Paul's secretary

__ 5. A talkative saint

__ 6. A business woman

__ 7. A hard-working woman

__ 8. First convert in Asia

__ 9. Paul's host

__ 10. A slaveholder

__ 11. A lady from Persia

__ 12. A red-haired Christian

__ 13. A delegate to Jerusalem

__ 14. A public official at Corinth

__ 15. Partners in tentmaking

A. Andronicus and Junia
B. Epaenetus
C. Erasmus
D. Gaius
E. Narcissus
F. Mary
G. Persis
H. Philologus
I. Phebe
J. Priscilla and Aquila
K. Rufus
L. Sosipater
M. Tertius
N. Tryphena and Tryphosa
O. Urbanus

FOOD FOR THOUGHT

"I do with my friends as I do with books. I would have them where I can find them but seldom use them."

—Ralph Waldo Emerson